MILESTONES OF FINANCIAL FREEDOM

Simple Steps For Conquering Debt And Building Wealth

By

Niyi Adeoshun

Nukan Publications

What Others Are Saying.........

Fantastic piece of work, easy to read and very practical. If you want to go from 'minus' to 'plus' in your life, then this book is for you. Prophet Isaiah told King Hezekiah "Put your house in order for you shall surely die"; the principles in this book will help you put order back into your finances and prevent financial ruin which can lead to premature death. This is a must on your bookshelf!!!"

Toyin O. Jama
Author of "Put Your Moses in the Basket"
Manchester, UK

This book should be in the hands of every credit card owner. Niyi's book is so critical for today's society because almost everyone has a credit card, racks up debt, and could easily fall into the debt trap, if you haven't already. Niyi gives you warning signs so that you know when you have to confront the situation fast, because it is easy to get into debt, and hard to get out of it. With this book – you have a real, step-by-step system for you to follow, that works. It's not a fun subject and for many who are looking for a quick fix – there isn't a magic wand for this, the fix starts with you and this book. By applying even one point in his emergency plan – you will pay for this book tenfold.

Tracy Repchuk
Bestselling author of "31 Days to Millionaire Marketing Miracles"
Burbank, California, USA

When I was presented with the manuscript of this book, I could not stop reading it until late into the night. As an international investor in financial instruments, I have never come across a book of this standard in both brevity and clarity. Niyi has avoided most financial jargons such as "Risk taker", "Risk neutral" and "Risk averse", and using plain English and real life situations, this book is truly second to none.

Reading the manuscript reminded me of the absolute necessity for self-discipline as quite rightly depicted in the book. A gentle man who worked in a financial institution in London, and earning over £100,000 per annum committed suicide after accumulating debts he could not service.

The step by step guides on financial management and the tables provided for financial planning are invaluable, and must be used meticulously to optimise the benefits of this book. You want to avoid debt trap, then read this book over and over.

Lawrence Abu
C.E.O. Liberty Financial & Accounting Services
International Investors in Financial Instruments and Real
Estate
London, UK

This book will undoubtedly leave you with only two obvious choices, one of both **admission and willingness to redress** your financial quagmire, strengthens any ongoing efforts if you are doing well financially or that of **defiance and nonchalant attitude** to say the least. This is because I find in this book little or no room for procrastination to anyone who dares to accept as compelling the facts and scriptural truth that are gradually but succinctly revealed.

Niyi has redefined the conventional idea of wealth creation from that of "get-rich-quick" scheme which has been the bane of our modern society, and sadly Christians also, to one of knowledge, creativity and hard work which he rightly tagged 'milestones' through which the cycle of indebtedness can be broken. Thus you will also find in this book a bridge and in-depth step by step directions you need to go from survivals to a stress-free financial life when followed diligently.

It is my privilege and honour to recommend this book to anyone and everyone who desires a life of financial freedom at such a low financial cost.

Emmanuel Dogo
Pastor, Dominion Chapel International
London, UK

This book is compulsory reading for our times. With the very unsettled financial climate, rising personal and national debt, a way of achieving freedom from debt and future financial stability for you (and generations to come) is a God-sent. Its common sense and storytelling format will make it an easy read for everyone.

Martin Adu
Christian Recording Artist
Leiden, Netherlands

Niyi has developed an interesting approach in his book and explores the gaps left behind or not thoroughly covered in the existing literature regarding meeting debt obligations and optimising saving habits.

The book is well written and entertaining and Niyi does a very good job of probing into individual financial obligations via a case study of a couple (Sally and Desmond Ellmas). He covers a variety of key areas in his book including: debt trap, money myths, creating a spending plan/emergency fund, meeting credit cards, consumer debt and mortgage repayment obligations. Towards the tail end he advises us how to teach our children about **'money management and achieving financial freedom'** these I found quite useful indeed.

I am impressed by the thorough and detailed approach of the book, but more impressed that he makes it easy and exciting to read for all and sundry irrespective of individual background/exposition. It is excellently written with no technical jargons and attains user friendliness.

I am delighted to recommend it to anyone who wants to have a better understanding of managing individual finances and investment.

Dr Bode Akinwande
Senior Lecturer in Financial Management
London Metropolitan University (London)

Getting out of debt is one of the biggest challenges and nightmares that a family can face and if not addressed can lead to all sorts of unforeseen consequences. Milestones of financial Freedom' not only outlines the stages of debt recovery in manageable and achievable stages but by basing the debt repair around issues faced by a family makes it very easy to relate to.

By breaking down the road to debt elimination into many small and achievable stages it means that progress can be measured and goals achieved all the way to the point where financial freedom is achieved. Many people think that debt is only an issue in the bad times but in fact managing debt in the good times is equally important so that if bad times do come then the issue will have been averted rather than magnified. **"Milestones to Financial Freedom"** offers practical help and guidance that nobody should ignore.

Mark Lofthouse
Former C.E.O. of Mortgage Brain Ltd
Bromsgrove, UK

With the current financial situation and the ongoing mismanagement of our finances, I cannot think of a better book to recommend. It is very easy to read, presenting a real-time view of how we manage our money and the warning signs we fail to notice or notice and choose to ignore. Financial freedom is an area of our lives which we all want to achieve this book will help you identify and address the financial areas of our lives which some of us have never thought of.

The financial management areas which are covered in this book are very clear and can be implemented by anyone; it presents a step by step guide making one think before spending, investing and planning.
 Great read!!!!

Antonia Iroko
Author, C.E.O. Projection Programmers
London, UK

Milestones of Financial Freedom
(Simple Steps For Conquering Debt and Building Wealth)

Niyi Adeoshun
http://www.niyiadeoshun.com

Published by Nukan Publications

Cover design by Adaku Oppong-Manu

Printed in the United Kingdom

First Edition: 2008
Second Edition: 2022

ISBN: 979-8-84-260906-2

Notice of Liabilities

The Publisher has strived to be as accurate and complete as possible in the creation of this book, notwithstanding the fact that he does not warrant or represent at any time that the contents within are accurate due to the rapidly changing nature of the financial world.

While all attempts have been made to verify information provided in this publication, the Publisher assumes no responsibility for errors, omissions, or contrary interpretation of the subject matter herein. Any perceived slights of specific persons, peoples, or organisations are unintentional.

This book is not intended for use as a source of legal, business, accounting or financial advice. All readers are advised to seek services of competent professionals in legal, business, accounting, and finance field.

Dedication

To all those who are determined to be financially-free so as to fulfil their God-ordained purposes on earth ....

... But especially to Joyce, my wife, lover, best friend, consultant and partner in life and its great adventures of becoming financially-free and fulfilling the will of God. Thank you for standing by me. I love you. ...

... And finally to our boys, Vincent, Christopher and David, who had to do with a little less 'Daddy-Time' while this project was in progress. You are all precious to me.

Acknowledgements

An African proverb says, "It takes a village to raise a child". For this book to get into your hands, it has taken the direct or indirect contributions of so many precious people.

I want to first of all thank God for making this book a reality by giving me the vision, strength and the dedication to accomplish it. Without Him I am nothing and can do nothing.

I wonder how much I would be able to accomplish without the prayers and godly advice of my parents, Peter and Folasade Adeoshun, which guided me in life and ministry. Thank you for believing in me.

My gratitude goes to the leadership and congregation of New Life Bible Church, Bethnal Green, London for giving me the opportunities to minister as well as hone my speaking and coaching skills in the church when I started teaching on Financial Freedom many years ago. Your questions, comments, suggestions, testimonies and encouragements have helped me to see this project to the end.

My thanks go to Tracy Repchuk, my Mentor and Coach in Internet business and an author herself, who encouraged and supported me from the beginning of this project by showing me steps that I would have otherwise missed out.

Special thanks also go to my good friend Antonia Iroko for lending her editing and proof-reading skills to this project. My reviewers Mrs Toyin O. Jama, Mark Lofthouse, Pastor Emmanuel Dogo, Pastor Lawrence Abu, Martin Adu, and Efua Quartey for their great work in making sure this book is published as well-polished as possible.

For their supply of the much-needed moral support before and during the period of the writing of this book I am grateful to the Akinsulires, the Williamses, the Alabis and the Olomofes.

Finally, I thank you all my clients and all those who have listened to me speak on financial freedom over the years. Your questions and suggestions have contributed in one way or the other to this project.

Foreword

Over the years I have often thought of the fact that the World with its present population of a little more than 6.5 billion, and given the fact that there are Billions and Trillions of pounds, dollars and other currencies in our Banks around the world – and in people's homes – why isn't everybody a millionaire? I believe that the world has enough resources provided by God for every human being to live comfortably on the Earth. Yet, it is evident that there are more poor people than the rich – not because there is no enough wealth to go round. We must be missing something somewhere.

I believe that there are principles God Himself has set in place to be applied in order to gain entry through the doors to true wealth. The world however, seems to have too many other ways of trying to make money, except the right ways. It is like the fact that the bigger the bunch of keys you are holding, the longer it will take you to figure out the right one to your door or car – **unless you have clearly marked out the right one**! This, I believe, is what Niyi has diligently helped to compress into this book – **marking out for us the right steps or "keys" to the doors to Financial Freedom – MILESTONES,** as he rightly calls them.

The book you hold in your hands, I believe, contains principles and bite-size ideas that will help every person that wants to be debt-free to begin the journey to financial freedom. The steps are both practical and relevant to our day to day living no matter your past or present circumstances. We might as well call them principles; or even laws – they will work for you, if they are properly put to work.

Going through the book, I have discovered that it is not one of those books that you buy just to read up a particular chapter or topic. Every chapter has very significant and integral steps to learn and apply, and like a dose of prescription drugs, they are better taken as prescribed – and over a period of time – for them to work. They are not just a quick-fix remedy to your situation. It took you time to get where you are that you don't like, it may take a while also to come out.

For the past over 13 years, I have observed Niyi carefully, and noted him to be a very meticulous and diligent man, both in spiritual things as a Church Elder, Director of Music, and as a family man. I am not surprised that he has come up with this wonderful work, full of insights and motivation. A book I would rather call a Manual. You may find some truths quite piercing because they nail your pride and put a check on that favourite habit of yours that led you to where you are today, but remember that sometimes you have to swallow a bitter pill to get well!

Get ready for a good read. Get ready to change or address some habits. Get ready to apply these steps. And get ready to experience financial freedom.

Rev. Richard Jama
Senior Pastor
New Life Bible Church, London

Table of Contents

Introduction

As a child and even as a young adult, school trips and holidays were events that I looked forward to – especially when it involved travelling long distances. My joy would be boundless if I got to sit by the window in the vehicle.

During the journeys, my face would be glued to the window – I just had to see the milestones; to see how far we had travelled and how many more miles (or kilometres) we had left to get to our destination. The closer we got to our destination, the more my excitement usually grew. It is this same kind of excitement that I want to generate in you through this book as you begin your journey to financial freedom.

In these days of road signs and route confirmation signs, you may be wondering; **"What is a milestone?"** I will give you a bit of history on the kind that I'm talking about here.

In ancient Rome, the Emperor Augustus placed a gilded pillar at the centre of the Forum, the *Millarium Aureum* (aka the Golden Milestone). The original golden milestone, raised in 20 BC, marked the starting point for a system of roads, all of which led to Rome. The roads were marked every mile (*mille* – Latin for 1,000 – the distance a Roman Legion covered in 1,000 paces) with a stone *"millarium"* or milestone.

The milestones had varied purposes:

- By them, travellers knew that they were actually on a Roman road, and these markers showed them just where in their travels they were in relation to Rome. *If you can see the milestones along your way, you can get to Rome.*

- Milestones are measures of progress (to the Romans, distance). The milestones in this book will show you how your journey to financial freedom is progressing. They are not your final goals but financial accomplishments which should be celebrated.

So when you start on your journey to financial freedom, think in terms of milestones along the way (indicators of progress) rather than the final goal (Total Financial Freedom) at the end of your journey, which can be overwhelming.

The steps detailed in this book may not make you rich overnight, but they will definitely help you sleep well at night.

> **"Your direction is more important than your speed."**
> - Richard L. Evans

To make this book easier to read, I have used a fictional couple, Desmond and Sarah Ellmas, whose progress we will follow as they attempt to become financially-free through simple but universally achievable steps recommended by their friend Craig Lamu.

This book, I pray, will provide you with the knowledge, inspiration, entertainment and encouragement that will prompt you to make the necessary adjustments to your financial situation in order to reach financial freedom.

Chapter 1

The Debt Trap

Sally held Desmond's gaze for a few seconds before looking away again as they both waited for the printer to stop its grinding sound. She then dropped her head - waiting for the bombshell. It was always her fault anyway she thought. Desmond gave a deep sigh, collected the printouts, moved away from the printer and walked towards Sally.

Without looking up Sally asked, "So what's the verdict?"

"Worse than we thought" Desmond replied.

He then went on to lay out the whole 'gloom and doom', holding nothing back and all the while pointing to figures on the sheets of paper. The time for pretence is long gone. Reality has hit home. This is not the time to play the 'blame-game' either.

For the Ellmases, this "financial meeting" is not like any they've ever had before. Actually, this was the first time they are really looking at all their outgoings on paper - together. Each time they talked about money in recent months, they usually ended up fighting and the meeting adjourned till another, more conducive time. Tonight though, there is not much left on any of the credit cards to borrow from again. So something has got to be done – and very quickly too!

This little scene above has been played out in different variations and in so many families in the past decade that it can no longer be ignored.

Debt is a problem; and for a lot of people, it is becoming their number one problem. From businessmen & women to career people, students and even old-age-pensioners (OAP), we all have a great tendency to buy and spend more than we should or can afford to do, which often leads to money management problems.

For the average family, there seems not to have been any other time in history when financial pressure is felt so overwhelmingly. For every penny they make, there are at least three major parties striving for it – the government, financial institutions and you (with your family) in the form of taxes, debt repayment and living expenses respectively.

Paying taxes (which is required) and monthly loan repayment has made people to appear as if they are just working to survive monthly without any hope of getting ahead in life.

The societies of today want us to believe that being in debt is the 'order of the day' or 'just the way things are'. They say 'everyone's doing it' and 'it doesn't matter because everybody borrows everyday'.

The UK credit statistics[1] (or should I call it debt statistics) as of April 2022 painted a frightening picture: -

- The average credit card debt per household in April 2022 was **£2,192**.

- The average total debt per household, including mortgages, was **£64,286**.

- Average owed by every UK adult, including mortgages, was **£33,780** (that is about 105.3% of average earning).

---

[1] https://themoneycharity.org.uk/media/June-2022-Money-Statistics.pdf

- Borrowers paid **£126 million** a day in interest in April 2022

- Total UK personal debt at the end of April 2022 stood at **£1,786.6bn.**

- According to the UK Office for Budget Responsibility's March 2022 forecast, household debt of all types is forecast to rise from **£2,019 billion** in 2020 to **£2,447 billion** in 2025!

For the fact that it takes about two to five years of subtle overspending before people start feeling uncomfortable about their finances, not many realise their debts are beginning to pile up. The question is "At what point should you start worrying about your debts"? If you are just "managing" on a monthly-basis, then perhaps you already have an unhealthy financial situation. Also, if ANY of the following statements is true, it is a warning sign that you're sliding - slowly but surely - into the financial bondage called debt:

- You are spending more than 20% of your monthly income on repaying your credit card and consumer debts.

- You are beginning to delay opening letters from financial institutions.

- You can only afford to make the minimum payments on your credit cards.

- You are using your credit card for day-to-day purchases without paying it off in full each month.

- Your credit card balances continue to increase.

- You apply for new credit cards **because** you don't have any money.

- You are juggling credit card payments, holding off one credit card to pay another.

- You find it hard to save even the smallest amount of money each month.

- You are taking out new loans to pay off old ones.

- Your total non-mortgage debt amounts to more than your annual income.

- You think you cannot 'afford' to pay tithe or give offering in church.

- You hide how much you are spending from your family and friends.

- You dip into your savings to cover non-emergency expenses.
  You have no way of paying for unexpected expenses like car repairs.

- You put off going to the doctor or dentist because you cannot pay the charges.

- Your application for a credit card or loan has recently been denied.

- You have considered filing IVA (Individual Voluntary Agreement) or even bankruptcy.

If any of the above is true, then you need to begin doing something about your indebtedness now!! If you are experiencing ANY of the warning signs above, then you could be heading for trouble. Hopefully, you are still in the early stages of debt at which you can take decisive and corrective actions that will be dealt with later in this book.

Reality Check

Desmond and Sally Ellmas have been married for about nine years and like all newly-weds they were full of hope and ambition. Their willingness to work together brought success, rewards and growth to them both as individuals and as a family. Later, in the process of acquiring 'stuff' for the house like furniture, the latest electronic gadgets in addition to two cars and exotic vacations, their finances began to slip from 'the straight and narrow'. They disguised their monthly overspending with the use of credit cards; buying whatever they wanted when they wanted them. This trend continued until these past few weeks when it finally dawned on them that they have 'maxed-out' all their four credit cards and they are actually way over their heads in debt. This in turn has led to the urgent family 'meeting' of this evening.

> "You don't drown by falling in the water, you drown by staying there."
> - Edwin Louis Cole

"What do we do now?" Sally asked, breaking the long and almost unbearable silence between them.

"We will be able to make the minimum payments on all the credit cards; use the payment holiday facility on the mortgage for this month, delay making the car payments by two weeks, reduce food shopping cash by £30 – then we will be okay. The situation now is that after this month if nothing changes, creditors will soon start calling on us." Desmond said in his usual analytical manner.

At this point, Sally began to sob saying "This has got to stop. We can't continue to live like this. We make more money than Barry and Joy next door but still we don't seem to get ahead in anything and now you are telling me we can't even afford to pay our mortgage?"

"Please don't start that again" Desmond said, his own frustration beginning to show. "You know, that may actually be part of our problem. We continually compare ourselves with anybody and everybody; trying to outdo them in everything; ours must be newer, better, bigger, faster, slimmer........." His voice trailed off when he realised that he has contributed more to this problem than Sally. His last sentence actually hit him like a sledgehammer when he remembered that he changed his mobile phone twice in the last 18 months just for him to show work colleagues that he has the latest handset available on his network.

Feeling anger beginning to rise due to his failure, mixed with absolute hopelessness, Desmond headed for the bedroom without saying another word. As he was leaving the living room, he remembered a quote by Mike Murdock that he learnt many years ago which says **"what you can tolerate, you cannot change"**. He admitted to himself that Sally was right and that things have got to change; but how?

Chapter 2

Money Myths

Sally woke up with a start the following morning to find Desmond rummaging through the box where they keep the birthday, anniversary pictures and Christmas cards precious to them.

"What are you doing?" she asked, sitting up on the bed.

"It's in the box. I know it's in here somewhere" Desmond mumbled to himself

"What is in the box?" she quizzed looking confused

"Craig's list" Desmond answered. "The one he gave us two years ago."

Craig Lamu, an Australian, has been friends with Desmond and Sally since their days at the University of Greenwich in London. They rekindled their friendship with Craig after they met at a reunion party two years ago. Unlike almost everyone else at the party, Craig seemed to be so sure of himself in everything he said that night. Though modestly dressed, a genuine aura of a high quality of life seemed to ooze from him. This made the Ellmases very curious and to ask him a lot of questions about what he was now doing for a living.

Craig was one of those people you would call 'average' in his college days. He didn't seem to exactly excel in anything but he usually got by somehow. The man the Ellmases saw at the reunion was a very different Craig – he was far above average in everything. They found out that he was once close to bankruptcy but came back from the edge of ruin to own a chain of retail sports shops in Southend, Birmingham, London, Manchester and also in three cities in Australia including Sydney.

When they met with him again for lunch the day after the reunion, they asked him for the 'secret of his success' like everyone else usually does, he wrote for them a list of the things he did to get out of debt and begin building wealth. The items on the list were so simple that Desmond threw the sheet of paper into the 'box' as soon as he read it just once. The 'box' is where the Ellmases have been putting items of sentimental value since they got married. Special birthday cards from friends went into it along with the pictures of their first holiday together as a couple along with other nostalgic things.

The reality of their financial situation as revealed last night prompted Desmond to dig out the list again.

"Here it is Sally. This is the list that Craig gave us two years ago, the day after the reunion party. I've kept it in the box ever since". Though deep down in Desmond's mind he knew he should have said *dumped* instead of *kept*. In any case he was glad he could still retrieve it at this point in time.

"How come we didn't think of it before now?" Sally asked holding the cream-coloured, A5-size piece of paper.

"It didn't seem like much then but after our 'discussion' last night, it came back to my mind and I just had to find it early this morning. So here it is and it still doesn't look like much."

"We'll need all the help we can get right now." Sally said beginning to read the content of the list. "There's got to be more to this list. These items are so simple that they can't be all that Craig did. Why don't we call Craig and ask him to explain the items on the list to us? It won't hurt to try."

"That's a good idea" Desmond said, already heading for the phone. "After all it is Saturday, let's just hope he hasn't gone on one of those his long holidays."

Craig picked up the telephone just on the second ring as he had just finished with another caller he has been mentoring in Australia but he was quite understanding in hearing what the Ellmases had to say. Sally narrated in details the situation of things and that they needed help with his 'list'.

"Welcome to the club guys" Craig said when Sally finished speaking "I see you've got to the stage I was seven years ago – congratulations!! You see, right after graduation, I wanted to get as many *big boy things* as I could in a short space of time before I 'settle down'. But before I knew it, I was up to my eyeballs in debt because I acquired ALL my stuff on credit and it got to a point I just could not make the monthly payment for them anymore. My so-called wife decided to leave at that point. I was only saved from bankruptcy when I found some buyers for my precious, non-essential household items and some personal 'bling-bling'.

"Even though I didn't know it at the time but millions of us are suffering from 'bling-itis' as we try to keep up with friends - the proverbial Joneses. Surveys show that about 70% of people aged 16 to 34 admitted to secretly competing with friends over expensive cosmetics, gadgets and clothes. Other age groups can be just as guilty as those above. What most people don't realise is that 'the Joneses' are also in debt.

"No one was there when I started struggling with debt-overload. I had to admit to myself that things had to change and to start to live within my means. Gaining control of my finances became my priority.

"Reality check is your first and most important step – without it, you will remain in the same financial state of 'never enough' until you get fed-up. You have to be sick and tired of the situation – sick of working just to pay debt and tired of not having much left to show for all your hard work. You must say to yourself 'enough is enough!' You must show that you are really serious before any turnaround can begin to take place."

Excuses and Myths

"Realising the seriousness of a situation is one thing, taking the appropriate actions is quite another. With all the credit problems that have been all around us in the last few years, one will think everybody will want to at least be debt-free. Sadly, this is not the case. When I ask people why they are in debt, not rich and not actively stepping towards financial freedom, I usually get answers like these:

- I just don't make enough (money)
- I'll get around to it later
- I deserve a little luxury in my life
- My interest charges aren't that much
- Spending makes me feel free!
- I was born into a poor family
- I need to support my family
- I am too young (or too old)
- I'm not smart enough
- I have no opportunities
- I lack the qualifications
- My spouse/parents will take care of it
- I have an unsupportive spouse

34

- I just have no luck

- The economy has been down

"Does any of these sound familiar to either of you?" Craig asked. When he didn't get an answer in any language he could understand, Craig continued. "The trouble with all these answers is that people tend to blame other people or something else for their financial situation. By so doing they are saying there's nothing they can do about their conditions. They would do better to rather address the habits which have created this financial bondage – taking full responsibility.

"Apart from these and other numerous excuses, the myths concerning money have helped the excuses of a lot of people to become realities in their lives. *"A **myth** is a traditional story that embodies popular beliefs or explains a practice, belief or natural phenomenon.*

"There are so many money myths floating around the world today that you will wonder if our society will ever be able to really discern between what is real and what is not. Here are a few of them:

1. My Stuff Is Mine

> Spend 10 minutes at a kindergarten or nursery school setting and you will surely hear the word 'mine, mine, mine' all over the place. Our selfishness begins right from babyhood. We have been taught to '**get all we can, can all we get and sit on the can**'. We usually think that what we have is ours to do with in any way we want without any level of caution. Only a small number of people have realised that all they own has been given to them by God for some specific purposes. *"The earth is the*

Lord's and its fullness thereof ..." the Bible says in Psalms 24:1. So if we use what is in our hands to do what God wants, our hands will always be full. Your stuff is not your; it is God's entrusted to you to do His will with.

2. All I need is a little more money

Can money solve money problems? I will say 'No'. Freedom from debt is not just a matter of money but a matter of habits. The more you earn the more your expenses usually become. If your spending, saving and investing habits don't change, more money will make little or no difference to your proposed financial   freedom.

According to Ecclesiastes 5:10 in the bible which says *"He that loves silver will not be satisfied with silver..."* more money is not the answer. If you don't manage or take care of what you have now, having more will make little difference.

3. I'm young, I still have time

Being young does not mean you can't start doing something about your financial future now. In fact, the earlier you start the better for you in the long run. It has been said that *the future comes one day at a time and time flies when you're having fun.* Soon you will be an adult with financial responsibilities; will you then be PREPARING for your future years or be REPAIRING the financial mistakes you are making now? The choice is yours.

4. Everything will be alright - somehow

Ignoring your debts won't make them go away. If you bury your head in the sand, sooner rather than later something (or someone) will come along and give you a big reality kick in the backside and it's going to hurt because you won't see it coming.

That kick could come from a creditor who you haven't contacted to work out an arrangement for payment of an outstanding debt; or possibly from a bank with a notification of a pending repossession of your house.

You need to face the facts that you have a problem and then set yourself goals to resolving it. Problems that are ignored, usually transform themselves into bigger problems a short way down the line. So today is the day that you need to start looking at your debts.

Taking action now can result in savings of interest and late payment fees. People who have money generally pay less than those who don't because they are able to pay debt on time and don't have to fund the additional expense of late payments in one form or another.

There is one thing that is certain and that is the fact that people who owe money might forget what they owe but those who are owed always know how much is due and when it is due, so you might prefer to forget but your creditors won't.

Also, more often than not a creditor will adopt a far more positive attitude towards you if you explain the situation you are in and let them know that you are currently working towards full and final payment of the debt as soon as possible.

Communication can do wonders for your debt reduction program. It will not work out somehow if you don't do anything about your finances.

5. I can win the lottery

Many people have been singing the 'lottery' song for a long time and they still have not won but instead are paying a 'voluntary tax' to the government. Even many of those who have won millions have gone out to buy all the 'bling-bling' they could lay their hands on - only to return to the same state they were before (if they are *lucky*).

Don't confuse financial freedom with wealth and asset. Financial freedom begins in the mind. You need to have a 'wealth mentality' to gain or retain wealth. Chasing 'free' lottery millions totally undermines the principle of biblical work ethics. 'Chance money' (gain through luck or gaming) is not what you want.

6. I can marry a rich person

We know ready-made meals are easier and faster to make than having to cook them from scratch. The drawback is that they don't taste exactly as you would have liked.

If your main reason of marrying someone is because the person is rich, you have already defined how far the marriage can go. Once its foundation (money) begins to get eroded, both the marriage and your financial freedom are doomed for failure.

7.   Money is the root of all evil

This statement is misquoting 1Timothy 6:10 in the Bible. The verse says *'The **love of** money is the root of all evil'*. Money, like fire, is a good servant but a bad master. You can have money and use it as a tool but don't turn it into an idol and let it have you.

"The great enemy of the truth is very often not the lie -- deliberate, contrived and dishonest -- but the myth -- persistent, persuasive and unrealistic"
-John F. Kennedy

"Okay, okay. We are guilty on all counts" Desmond said, when Craig finally stopped speaking.

"We have used all the excuses and we have also believed most of the myths you mentioned as the truth - until now." Sally continued where her husband stopped. "The result has not been pretty as you can see. Craig we need help. Can you help us?"

"Of course, I will and there is no point in you *re-inventing the wheel*. I have gone through what you are going through now and I have come out victoriously on the other side by following some simple, achievable and consecutive steps. Notice that I said 'simple steps' and not 'easy steps'; what we will be doing will go against what you've been used to and that's where the difficulties may lie.

39

"If you are ready to do what I ask of you, I may be able to walk you right out of this situation that you are in now. Is that okay?"

"Yes. That's fine. We're ready. We've got nothing to lose" Desmond replied "When do we start?"

"In a few minutes. Aren't you lucky?" Craig replied with sarcasm in voice.

"What? You're not serious Craig...."

"Yes I am" Craig said quickly "I have discovered that when people get to this stage that you are now and they don't start on their journey to financial freedom right away, they tend to just drift back to what they've been used to. So be ready to drop some of your current habits and pick up some new ones starting from today. I have stopped procrastinating about financial matters for many years now and you will need to do that in order to gain the freedom that you seek.

"Get some writing materials; I will call you right back. Just give me a few minutes to quickly sort some things out here." With that Craig put the phone down, leaving the Ellmases to get their writing materials and get comfortable with their coffee mugs at their kitchen table.

Chapter 3

What You See Is What You Get

The next fifteen minutes were some of the longest that Desmond and Sally Ellmas have had to endure. While waiting, they discussed the changes they observed in Craig when they met him at the reunion at The Clarendon Hotel, London. Craig talked like someone who had pursued a dream with persistence and had succeeded, but still he planned to perfect some outstanding expectations with the same courage. The results in his life spoke for themselves. Though not flashy, but everybody knew he was 'loaded' (that's *wealthy* for the uninitiated).

Craig had always been a clean-living kind of person so they knew he couldn't have been involved in anything shady. He would not let anything compromise his Christian integrity. He was also as strong-headed as they come. He wasn't very easy to convince about most things; but once he made up his mind about something, it would equally take a miracle to change it. The Ellmases listened with huge interest to all Craig told them about what he did to become financially free though they thought that wasn't for them as they were, in their own eyes, financially secure – until now.

Both Sally and Desmond reached for the phone when it finally rang. Desmond answered it and put Craig on speakerphone as he did earlier.

"Are you guys sure you really want to get out of debt? The reason I'm asking this is because I have dealt with some people who said they wanted to be debt-free only for me to find out later that they were only just wishing, hoping, wanting or even just desiring. They were ready to enjoy the rewards of being financially-free without the willingness to be disciplined and be committed to what must be done.

"Make a commitment now that you will achieve financial freedom; because your decision will definitely bring many inconveniences into your lives – for a little while. If you set your focus firmly on financial freedom, you will be able to bear whatever temporary inconveniences you encounter. There is no freedom without sacrifice."

"Craig, believe me Bro, we are ready to go all the way" Desmond assured him. He has reached the financial turning point in his life.

"In that case, let's make a start" Craig replied, with equal enthusiasm.

The Dream

"Since you're both computer-literate, I'll begin with what you already know" Craig began. "WYSWIG (*What You See Is What You Get*) is not just 'computer-speak'; it is 'financial-freedom-speak' as well. The world we live in has clouded the visions of a lot of people. The world says "debt is a way of life" and people believe it. Well, debt may be the way of most people's lives but does that necessarily make it true for YOU? Have you ever 'seen' yourself debt-free?"

"In our current financial state - No" Sally replied emphatically.

"It is possible that you slid into this financial bondage like most people, but it is highly unlikely that you will just slide out

42

again. Your freedom must start in your mind. To get out of debt, you must see yourselves out of debt.

"Alright guys, put debt and financial difficulties aside for a moment and follow me to the 'imagination station'. Imagine that this month you don't have to pay creditors ANYTHING. A house without the mortgage, cars without the car payments; also no credit card or loan payments either. Your Aunt Sue has also (finally) received back the money she lent to you 5 years ago – thank God! How will you feel if all you have to spend money on are only the monthly essentials?"

"That would be like heaven! You won't believe it, but I'm already feeling so good just thinking about it" Sally said, grinning for ear-to-ear at Desmond.

"I can get used to a life like that Craig. No more?! Wow!!" Desmond added excitedly.

"I'm glad you guys are excited about that. But seriously speaking, in a situation like that... peace... great peace is what you will have and that is what you are feeling already Sally. You will then be able to think clearly about how you will fulfil your God-ordained purpose(s) on earth – and believe me we all have one, we just don't seem to get round to it. Some people, sadly, never will."

> **"Imagination is the beginning of creation. You imagine what you desire; you will what you imagine; and at last you create what you will"**
> - George Bernard Shaw

"Now I want you to dream for a little while about what you actually want to accomplish in and with your lives. In an ideal situation, what you would like to be or have? Remember that if you have money, you have options. You can be a rich volunteer somewhere, have a big house – if you wish, lots of cash, nice cars, big successful businesses, rental properties, go on a once in a lifetime holiday, send your children to the best universities, sponsor a child in a Third-World country etc. What you are now using is your vision.

"Vision captures something that is not actually visible yet. It is an invisible picture of your future. Frankly speaking, everybody has vision but most people don't have the right one. Some can only remember the past – they use memory as if it were vision; some can't see past their current situations; only very few people are looking favourably ahead. What you see is what you get. If you can see better, you can get better."

Set Goals

"Whatever you are seeing now can become your goals which will give you focus as you aim for financial freedom. It is necessary to define your goals as either being short-term or long-term depending on the length of time it will take to accomplish that goal. A short-term goal is something you can accomplish in less than five years such as paying off credit cards or loans or saving for emergencies. Long-term financial goals however can be saving for your children's university education or retirement.

"By defining your goals, you are taking control of your finances and this will be our starting point today. You now have something to aim for. Your goals will give you direction, drive, as well as the discipline to stay on course."

As if on cue, the Ellmases' fax machine started receiving a document. Craig on hearing the fax machine said "That, my friends, is the document you will use to write your goals – both short-term and long-term *(see appendix A)*. I have discovered that writing down your goals crystallises your thinking and promotes you to take the appropriate action. You both need to write down, together, those things that are important to you; that you want to accomplish. As a rule, make sure the goals are specific, measurable, achievable, relevant and time-bound. If you don't put as specific time to it, you are bound to start relaxing again singing the *"There's Still Time"* song. Identify your goals clearly and why they matter to you, and decide which are the most important. By concentrating your efforts on those, you have a better chance of achieving what matters most."

> **"Vision without action is a daydream.**
> **Action without vision is a nightmare."**
> – Japanese proverb

"For many people, knowing how to start on the journey to financial freedom is really a nightmare, because they just cannot see a way out of their present predicament. The reason for this is most of the time, they are looking for a clear way from where they are right now to where they want to be – that is financial freedom.

"Imagine yourselves intending to travel from London to Birmingham, it will be foolish of you to wait for all the traffic lights to 'turn green' before to start out! No, you won't do that. You will have to make the journey one traffic light at a time; one road at a time; until you reach your destination. This is how I would like to take you on this your journey to financial freedom. We will take it one stage or **one milestone at a time**. The whole idea is to divide the journey into short hops so it won't feel long and boring but in short, simple, achievable and exciting stages. Exciting because each milestone you reach brings you closer to your destination and should be celebrated. When you know you are on the right path what remains then is *how quickly* you want to reach your destination."

The Journey Begins

"If you want something like freedom from debt badly enough, you must be willing to pay the price. Based on the information you have given me Desmond, you guys seem ready to do whatever it takes to be debt-free and to start building wealth progressively. As I have promised to help, I want to take you through the requirements of each milestone. One Saturday every month or so for the next few months we will have a session, is that okay with you guys?"

"No problem at all" answered Desmond.

"Here we go. To begin with, let's imagine your financial situation as a ship in the middle of the ocean. You have just found out that you are going in the wrong direction and you know you need to turn around. The bigger your ship is, the longer it will take you to turn it around. Don't worry about the duration just bear in mind that very soon you will be going towards your desired destination.

"The first thing you need to do is to STOP, cut the engine and do not add any more distance or else it will take you even longer to get back to your desired destination.

> "You can't solve your problem by continuing in the
> process that created it."
> – Edwin Louis Cole

"You need to stop accumulating more debt. Do not add any more DEBT to your financial situation or else your ship will hit a giant iceberg pretty soon – just like the Titanic.

Net Worth

"Next you need to find out where your ship is in reference to where you want to go – your desired destination.

"You need to find out where you are at the moment financially. To do this, you need to calculate what your Net Worth is. Your Net Worth is what is left after you've subtracted all you OWE i.e. your liabilities (loans, credit cards, mortgages etc.) from the *current cash value* of all you OWN i.e. your assets (properties, stock, bond, cars, jewelleries, cash in bank etc).

"If you own more than you owe, you have a positive net worth. This is a good thing; but how much your ideal Net Worth should be, depends on your personal circumstances. For a general idea of what your net worth should be, based only on your age and income, it is sometimes suggested that you multiply your annual income by your age and divide by ten. Note that this is just simply an average and doesn't take specific personal situations into account.

"If, on the other hand, you owe more than you own, then you have a negative net worth. This is not a good thing at all, but it is information you need to know so as to gear up quickly and at least make the Net Worth positive as soon as possible.

Debt to Income (DTI) Ratio

"One measure of financial health very popular with mortgage lenders of today is the Debt to Income ratio. Your debt-to-income ratio is a personal finance measure that compares the amount of money that you earn to the amount of money that you owe to your creditors. For most people, this number comes into play when they are trying to line up the financing to purchase a home, as it is used to determine mortgage affordability. You too can calculate it for yourselves just to get a better picture of your financial situation. *(See Appendix B)*

"Some Debt-to-Income calculations include your mortgage or rent and others don't. I like to use the former which includes the total amount of money that you spend each month servicing debt because it gives a better overall picture. This includes all recurring debt payments, such as mortgages, student loans, child support payments, credit card payments, car and other consumer loans. When calculating this ratio, don't count monthly expenses such as food, entertainment and utilities – just what you owe creditors.

Debt-to-Income Ratio = (Total Monthly Debt Payments Divided by **Total Monthly Income)** Multiplied by **100%**

"Most lenders will tell you that a 36% or lower debt to income ratio is good. In reality, it's difficult to apply a one-size-fits-all formula to everybody. Your personal situation, such as number of dependents, unusual expenses, and spending habits will affect how much debt you can reasonably handle, but as a

48

general guideline, let's assume that anything over 36% would be uncomfortable for the average person.

"You can gauge your current situation with the following statements. If your debt to income ratio is:

- Less than 30%: Excellent! (But the ultimate aim is 0%)

- 30% to 36%: Good. You won't have any problem with lenders, but work to bring it down below 30% and then aim for 0%

- 36% to 40%: Borderline. Some lenders will still give you a loan but you may struggle to make your payments.

- 40% or higher: Red flag. Your debt situation requires very urgent attention.

"From what you've told me, I think the red flag is beginning to fly on your finances. Please note that we are NOT doing this exercise so you can go and borrow more money. We are doing it to find out exactly where you are financially. You cannot, by the way, borrow your way out of debt. Borrowing money should be off your agenda for now at least.

Spending Diary

"In addition to the above, I would like you to write down everything you spend money on in the next 30 days as well as how much they cost - no matter how small. I will be emailing you a sample of the form *(See Appendix C)* you will use to log your daily spending. Just print as many copies as you require.

"Are these exercises as you call them not too much for one session?" Desmond asked 'innocently'.

"No my friend, these exercises are necessary. They are like the data you feed first into a GPS (Global Positioning System) that will be used to locate your position – only on this occasion it is your financial position. You can only manage what you can measure. So these measurements we are trying to do are crucial to what comes after this session.

"Oh like the Satnav cars, right?" Desmond said, almost like a student who just understood a new mathematical formula.

"You got that right" Craig replied.

"I know it's going to be an absolute pain having to write down every single penny you spend on a day-to-day basis and it may seem a bit pointless when it's only 45p for a can of Pepsi-Cola or a bar of Snickers (my favourites). But that's the whole point of this exercise! I believe that keeping a diary is a very effective way of helping anybody who is trying to become financially-free to bring his/her spending under control. Somehow, it seems to bring home the true value of money when you've got a piece of paper in front of you telling you where your entire income for the month went.

"You're going to be surprised (if not shocked) to find that you spend a fair bit on the small things. Sandwiches, coffee, spur-of-the-moment pub lunches, impulse buys and frequent trips to the corner shop for drinks and nibbles on the way home to (and from) work. It all mounts up and hurt your pocket in the long run as well. You don't stumble on big rocks; it is the small stones you need to watch out for."

Craig allowed his last sentence to sink in for a few moments, he then informed them saying "I am off to Australia next week but I'm sure you have enough to do before we speak again next month. By then your goals would have been set as the focus; you would have calculated your Net Worth, your Debt to

Income ratio and we will have an idea of your spending pattern. I call that a good start, don't you?

"Yeah, right. Easy for you to say" Desmond replied

"Safe journey. We'll be ready with our data by the time you return from Australia Craig." Sally said, trying to sound like a better student than Desmond.

God Force One

"One more thing" Craig added "and this is very important. Just as you have called me for help, invite God also into your financial situation. I myself depend on God for the wisdom that I am and will be passing on to you. Most folks tend to leave God out of their financial crisis when they should be running to Him in the first place. The earlier He is invited in, the better – though with God no situation is ever too hopeless or too late. Just remember, the steps of the righteous are ordered by God.

"Just as those specifically configured, highly customised Boeing 747-200B series aircrafts are referred to as 'Air Force One' only while the American president is on board; so will your financial situation become '**God Force One**' when God is on board. The rules however, will change when God is in the situation with you. How you earn, spend, save, give, invest etc must be in line with the will of God. Think about that and I'll talk to you again next month."

Craig concluded the conversation knowing (and satisfied) that he had left his friends with plenty of 'food for thought' while at the same time he had started them on the road to their financial freedom.

51

Chapter 4

Where There Is a Will ...

Saturdays have always been Desmond's day to lie-in and today is not supposed to be an exception. It was however, only a few minutes after six when the telephone started ringing; Desmond somehow struggled out of bed to answer it. Craig was at the other end. Desmond guessed Craig must have either forgotten the time difference between Sydney and London or his house was on fire. This was not even the last Saturday of the month; that's still two weeks away.

"Hello Bro" Craig started in his usual cheerful manner. "I hope I have managed to wake you up."

"Craig do you know what time it is?"

"Desmond, I had to wait for three whole hours before placing this call so I'm actually doing you a favour. You should be thankful I didn't call you at 3am. Is Sally awake yet?"

"No" Desmond replied.

"Okay" Craig said. "I might as well get this off my chest now. I need to ask you an important question. Give me the right answer and you can go right back to bed; otherwise consider yourself awake for the day" to which Desmond quickly answered "Fire on" hoping to continue sleeping within the next minute or two.

"Do you have a Will Desmond? I mean 'Last Will and Testament'"

Desmond replied "Am I not too young to be thinking about that?"

Craig pressed on with "So you don't have a Will. Am I right?"

"No, I don't – not yet anyway" Desmond replied still wondering what this has got to do with his Saturday morning.

"Do you love your family?" Craig continued after a few seconds.

"Of course I do" Desmond replied defensively.

"Desmond my friend, you seem to have put yourself in the category of the 'carefree' people with dependants living 'dangerously' without a written Will. Research has shown that three quarters of people in the UK have yet to write a Will *(figures may be slightly different in other countries)*. Surveys also suggest that one-third of the people surveyed do not want a Will or feel they don't need one. Meanwhile, about one quarter think leaving an inheritance could cause problems among relatives over how the family divides the estate; so their philosophy is - no inheritance, no need for a Will. On the other hand, almost 40% expect to leave an inheritance of up to £300,000 while 18% expect to leave more than this, a study says.

"With lots of people still contemplating whether to have a Will or not, some people already believe a local hospital should receive the money when the person who died has no dependents while others believe the homeless or local schools should receive it. But who should decide what happens to the wealth YOU worked hard for? If you don't have a Will and you die intestate (that is - dying without a legal Will), you don't have a say in it.

> **"A good man leaves an inheritance to his children's children, and the wealth of the sinner is stored up for the righteous"**
> Proverbs 13:22 (The Bible)

"Like you, almost everybody knows it is important to make a Will, but most people put off making one of their own for a variety of reasons. Here are some of the top excuses people make:

Excuse: "I've just been much too busy to think about it"
If your loved ones are important to you, you need to create the time to make the Will - unless you are just working for the government!!

Excuse: "I can't make up my mind what I want to put in it"
If you don't, the government will decide for you - if that's what you want. Make a Will now, you can always change it later.

Excuse: "My spouse just doesn't want to talk about it"
I understand that some people believe that if they don't have a Will, they will live forever. Having a Will, on the other hand, will not kill you. If your spouse doesn't want to talk about is it, why don't you make your own Will? You need one too!

Excuse: "We can't agree about who we want as guardians"
A not-too-comfortable decision is better than no decision at all! Why not have your choice of guardians in your Will and your spouse's choice in his/her Will? Just pray the two of you don't *give up the ghost* at the same time – as this may lead to the clash of the guardians.

Excuse: "Our assets are constantly changing"
So? What's the delay? It would be even harder if something happened to one of you while the change is in progress. Make the Will now; you can always amend it later.

"Desmond, no one likes to think about death, dying or what happens when they die. But if we don't, our families could suffer. Financial hardship and worry are not the ideal legacy for a family mourning the loss of a loved one.

"Making a Will is relatively stress-free and not expensive if your financial situation is straight-forward like most people's. In the absence of a signed Will for those living in England and Wales (rules vary from country to country), the government dictates **who** gets **what** of your estate, depending on your domestic circumstances. Here are the current rules as to who gets what:

Married or in Civil Partnership with Children[2]
(separated people are treated under these rules as still being married)

- Your spouse keeps all the assets (including property), up to £270,000, and all the personal possessions, whatever their value.
- The remainder of the estate will be shared as follows:
- Your spouse gets an absolute interest in half of the remainder
- the other half is then divided equally between the surviving children
- If a child (or other child where the deceased had a parental role) has already died, their children will inherit in their place.

Married or in Civil Partnership with No Children but with Parents and/or Brothers and Sisters
Your spouse will receive all personal possessions and the proceeds of the estate.

---

[2]. https://www.gov.uk/inherits-someone-dies-without-will

Married with No Children and No Parents or Brothers and Sisters

Your spouse gets everything.

Unmarried with NO children

The entire estate will go to the following relatives, in this order:

- Their parents;

- If parents are deceased, to their brothers and sisters (with full siblings coming before half-siblings);

- If they have no siblings or surviving parents, to their grandparents;

- If grandparents are also deceased, to uncles and aunts or their children.

Single, Widowed or Divorced (but not separated)

Everything goes to your children (if any), otherwise to your parents (if alive), otherwise to your brothers and sisters (or their children), otherwise your grandparents (if alive), otherwise your uncles and aunts (or their children), otherwise to the government!

"You don't want your estate to be treated like government property or to cause the totally breakdown of the loving relationships your dependants currently have - do you Desmond? The point is, if you don't plan for what happens to your stuff after you die, someone else, who does not know or care about your wishes, ideals, faith, family needs etc. may have to make them for you - according to the law. A judge who doesn't know or care about your family values can choose guardians for your children if they are still minors when you pass away."

"I am not being legalistic here; I am talking about love. Love your family enough to provide for them now and later when you start 'singing in the heavenly choir'.

"Thank you Craig for bringing that up" said Sally who woke up wondering who Desmond was speaking to early in the morning. Desmond pressed the speaker button to allow her hear what Craig was saying.

"Hi Sally. Thanks for joining us. I'm sorry for calling you guys so early in the morning."

"How did you boys get round to such a subject like this so early in the morning anyway?" Sally asked curiously.

"I got bored so I thought I would wake my friends in England up. From the look of things, I think I've succeeded; ha, ha, ha" Craig laughed "Seriously speaking this is quite important and I haven't been able to get it off my mind since last week when I left England. So I just called to get it off my chest considering my own experience."

"By the way Sally, you need a Will too you know. Either of you can 'kick the bucket' first; the whole idea is not to let what you've both worked hard for fall into the hands of the government or some greedy relatives or become tied up because of family legal issues.

"The easiest way is for you guys to have what is called Mirror Will. A Mirror Will is prepared when a couple want to make almost identical Wills leaving, for example, everything to each other respectively and thereafter to the children, or where there are no children, to a named beneficiary. They must be individual Wills; separate legal documents but with similar content. The respective partners usually become both sole beneficiary and sole executor to each other.

"When writing a Mirror Will in this way it is essential to add at least one extra executor to each Will to safeguard the estate in the event that the couple should depart this life together. The second executor can be the same person in both Wills, or you may choose to have different executors. However, naming different guardians in your Wills could lead to problems especially if you both *answer the silent trumpet call* at the same time.

"By having a Will, you will be able to:

- Save your dependants a lot of trouble, expense and delay after you're gone
- Appoint a guardian for your children
- Make financial provision for your children's upkeep and education
- Make sure there are no arguments over who gets what in the family
- Make sure your family or spouse's family don't get everything leaving the children destitute if you both go to meet your Maker together
- Avoid the situation where the government or anyone else will decide who gets what
- Prevent your home from being sold while someone in your family still needs it
- Make provision for an elderly or handicapped relative so the government doesn't take it all

Life Insurance

"What about Life Insurance Desmond, do you have that?"

When Desmond answered with a grunt, Craig was about to continue with his 'love talk' when Sally broke in.

"You're not holding anything back at all today Craig, are you?" she said somehow bemused by this early-morning 'bombardment'.

"No Madam. When you've just lost a loved one, the last thing you want to think about is how to keep a roof over your head, put food on the table, keep the lights on or put fuel in the car. Why should you (the dead) be enjoying in heaven while your dependants (the living) are going through hell on earth?"

"Believe me Craig, I have been meaning to get to that. It has just been slipping my mind" Desmond finally responded.

"Your twins are almost 8 years old!! When will you get round to it?" Craig quizzed.

"With the financial situation we have at present, we just can't seem to find more money for that" Desmond answered already feeling embarrassed.

Craig would not let up. "'That', my friend, may be what stands between your family and poverty when you, the main breadwinner, starts 'pushing up daisies'. Don't get me wrong, I understand the situation of things right now but some things cannot just be left undone. That is why I just have to call you today".

"But Craig, there are so many different kinds of life insurance policies out there. How do we know which one is best for us?" Sally queried.

"The life insurance you will require will depend on a number of factors such as your age, gender, occupation, state of health, whether you smoke or not, the amount of cover, the length of the policy etc. You just need to choose which one will suit you best out of the whole lot. I agree it can be a daunting task choosing one but once you have even a basic understanding of insurances, you will be in a better position when making your decision.

"Life insurance is essentially a protection for you, your family and your lifestyle. This protection is usually referred to either as **in**surance or **as**surance.

- **Insurance** protects you against something that *might* happen e.g. dying during the term of a policy.

- **Assurance** protects you against something that is *sure* to happen e.g. dying!!

"I hope you are beginning to see some light inside the life insurance 'cave'.

"Yes go on, go on" Desmond urged him.

"Anybody who is a breadwinner (main or supplemental) in a family setting or has a spouse or other dependants needs a life insurance policy. The trick is in knowing how much to insure yourself for; you don't want to either be over-insured or be under-insured. Your insurance pay-out should, at the very least, leave your family free of debt when you die and still live at their current standard but your death should not be like a lottery-win for your family either because you over-insure. You don't want to be seen as being worth more dead to your family than when you are alive!! On the other hand, you don't want to put them in the 'poor house' at your death either. So you need to balance things out properly.

"To give your dependants a reasonable standard of living, many financial experts recommend that you need to get insured for about eight to ten times your current gross annual income.

"Another factor to consider is how long your life insurance policy should be for? I usually tell people to let their policies cover them until their children are old enough to be financially stable. That's normally about the age of twenty-five. Another criterion to use is to get covered until your normal retirement age of at least to sixty-five.

"There are two main types of life insurance policies that are sold most by insurance companies (apart from the mortgage life insurance which pays off mortgage if you die during the term of the mortgage). These are the Term Life Insurance and the Whole of Life Insurance.

"I prefer term-life insurance to whole of life insurance. The reasons are already in their definitions below:

- **Term Life Insurance** is the simplest form of life insurance. Generally speaking, you pay same premium for the term of the policy and if you die during the term, it pays out a cash lump sum.

- **Whole of Life policies** cover the whole of your life – meaning it pays out regardless of when you die. These are more expensive than term life policies and they are often not necessary for many people. Your dependants won't really need it once they become financially stable.

"Have I managed to answer your question Sally?" Craig asked, as if in conclusion.

"Sure. We have no excuse now" Sally replied.

"There's still the question of where I will find the extra money to pay for this" Desmond said, bringing everybody back to the present.

"Let me see.... uh, I know you still play golf and you've tried many times to talk me into joining a Golf club in the past. I'll love to play myself but I just don't have the time right now. Why don't you use your membership fee to pay the life insurance premium for a few months until things get better financially?"

"W-W-W-What?!" Craig stuttered in disbelief.

"Whoa! Calm down Des. It is just a suggestion. Help me out here Sally" Craig said, waiting for 'Sally the Great' to mediate between them as usual.

"Craig's on to something, Darling" Sally said trying to sooth her husband but deep down she was over the moon at the suggestion.

"Yeah, Craig is *on something* alright...." Desmond grumbled, knowing this is one argument he won't be able to win. Then turning to his wife, he said "... and Sally, you are supposed to be on my side."

"I am, my love, I am" Sally laughed, patting Desmond on the back.

"All the same Desmond" Craig continued, trying not to lose his train of thoughts. "Look at it this way, which one do you love more - your family or your golf? Personally, I don't think any activity should take precedence over the survival of your beloved family."

"Now, you're not being fair Craig."

"I know … and I like it, my friend" Craig said trying to keep a straight face.

"So what am I supposed to do in the meantime?" Desmond asked, desperately looking for a way out of his 'no golf' sentence.

"What you always do. Watch the Golf channels on TV. You might even learn something new this time" Sally suggested.

"... and be close enough to the kitchen to wash some dishes" Craig added.

"... and just be at home on Saturday afternoons! Hallelujah!!" Sally said excitedly and mocking Desmond at the same time.

"Alright, alright, I've got the picture. I'll do whatever needs to be done – even if it kills me." Desmond surrendered.

"You may have withdrawal symptoms for a few weeks but you won't die" Sally assured him.

"Neither will you Sally, when you use the fees for your aerobics classes for your own life Insurance premium." Craig said as gently as he could break the news to her.

"Desmond, I thought this guy is supposed to be YOUR friend" Sally said.

"Yes he is and I like him even more by the minute now" Desmond said laughing at his wife's 'do-your-aerobics-at-home' agony.

"I'd better let you guys 'enjoy' your Saturday morning" Craig said quickly before Sally could find anything to say. "I guess my work for today is done. I hope the life insurance policies will be ready by the time we meet again. Please set the ball rolling today on the Wills as well. Remember where there's a will, there's always a way" Craig said sounding like a doctor who's giving his patients some final instructions that he doesn't want them to forget.

Milestone #1

Create a Spending Plan

Chapter 5

The Spending Plan

It has been two weeks since Craig's early morning call from Australia. This is his first full session with the Ellmases. After they have exchanged all the customary pleasantries, Craig got ready to start towards the first milestone which is – creating a Spending Plan. So he asked his friends a question out of the blues:

"How do you eat an elephant?" Craig asked the Ellmases.

"With fork and knife of course" Desmond answered laughing more at his own quick and witty response than the question from Craig.

"With a cutlass and garden fork will be more like it. Even with those, it will take a long time to finish the beast", Sally added.

"The main idea is just to finish it - no matter how long it takes" Craig said. "**You eat an elephant one bite at a time**. Before you can say 'Jungle book', you've finished it. Trying to gulp it down all in one go will cause serious indigestion amongst other things. I won't put it past Desmond to have a go at doing just that.

"Ha-ha-ha; very funny" said Desmond

"The elephant here may represent your Financial Freedom and the bites will be the milestones which we will be aiming for as we go through this journey. You need to celebrate each milestone you reach, no matter how subdued the celebration may be. The duration for reaching each milestone will vary and so will your celebration. Your creditors will not be rejoicing for letting you slip from within their grasp so you have to do it yourselves and within reason. Okay?"

"Okay", the Ellmases chorused.

> **"The plan of the steadily diligent tends to plenty ..."**
> Proverbs 21:5 (The Bible)

Create a Spending Plan

"Planning is what you do to easily and successfully get from point A to point B. Nothing works the way you want it to if you don't do anything about it. You've got to plan for your freedom.

"Personal finance is so personal that it affects your whole person (physically, spiritually, logically, psychologically, etc) now and in the future. Your finances comprise of your earning, spending, saving, giving, investing and so on. When spending turns into over-spending, a not-so-little problem called Debt might occur which will require some planning on your side to solve.

"Lenders have plans and advertisers also have plans to get as much of your money as they can legally get or as much as you can allow them. They have never looked out for your best interest and they never will. They are in business to make money – from you - in small monthly payments. If you don't make your own plan to get out from under the weight that debt has put you, you might as well just be working for your creditors for the rest of your lives." Craig said frankly.

"No matter how much you earn; you need a budget. Don't even try to get by without a budget as you will be setting yourself up for failure. It's as simple as that. Running personal or family finance without a budget is like driving a car with a faulty fuel gauge – sooner or later your empty petrol tank will leave you at the side of the road. Without a budget you can't hope to have control over your finances.

"If you're like most folks, by now, hearing the word '**BUDGET**' over and over would have started making you quake in your financial boots. The term 'budget' is perceived to mean limitation, restriction, deprivation or doing-without just as we think 'starvation' wherever someone mentions the word 'diet'.

"From now on I will be using the term '**Spending Plan**' instead of budget. This is because a plan indicates progress and forward thinking and is like a guide that, in this case, will help you take control of your financial future and, ultimately, reach your other goals. The Spending Plan is a plan or schedule adjusting expenses during a certain period to the estimated or fixed income for that period. It is the plan you make on paper on how to spend your COMING income in real life.

"This plan:

- will help you live within your means
- will help you spend on only the things that matter
- will help you get out and stay out of debt
- will help you become more aware of how much money you are unnecessarily spending each month
- will free up extra money for you to use
- may even improve your marriage as you both now have to be on the same page regarding your needs, wants and desires.

"If someone were to ask you both six weeks ago to write down exactly how much it costs you to live day to day, week to week, and month to month -- could you have come up with the figures? Since our last meeting things have changed I'm sure. Honestly speaking, before now you would probably have to admit that it would take quite some time as you would have to look through your credit card statements, monthly bills, shopping receipts etc. to get a clear picture of how much money you are spending. In addition to that you would have needed to look at any expenses that occur at irregular intervals such as quarterly or annually.

"Your first Spending Plan will be created historically from your past spending pattern. That is why I asked you last month to start itemising everything you spent money on each day in the last 30 days. Use the results from the various categories together with your normal monthly payments which you can get from your bank statements to create your Spending Plan.

"Your Spending Plan can be very simple, or very detailed. People with a larger income (and expenditure) tend to have more detailed Spending Plans, but people with modest income and outgoings will usually do well with a simplified one.

"Your Spending Plan can be written out on paper, typed in a document or spreadsheet on your computer, or set up in a money management program on your computer. Whatever works best for you and your situation should be used; just don't make it more difficult than it has to be. Whatever the case, it should be easily editable. The reason I'm saying this is that your spending Plan, as in most cases, will need to be adjusted a lot over the first few months for it to work well."

"There are four basic steps that you must take when creating your spending plan:

70

1. List Your Income.

This is the easiest part of the Plan as most people have very few sources of income. Be sure to include all income that you know will be coming in, including bonuses, overtime, rental income, business incomes, commissions, child support, benefits, even income tax refunds and cash gifts that you know you will receive from Grandma at Christmas.

It is possible that you receive some of your income weekly, fortnightly, monthly etc; make sure all the figures are for the same period (don't mix up weekly and monthly figures: this might seem basic, but the important thing is that you get it right). As most payment cycles used nowadays are monthly, use the calculations below to determine the average monthly income for your non-monthly income:

- If you are paid weekly, multiply your weekly pay by 4.333

- If you are paid fortnightly, multiply your fortnightly pay by 2.167

- If you are paid semi-monthly, multiply your semi-monthly pay by 2

- If you are paid quarterly, divide your quarterly pay by 3

- If you are paid bi-annually, divide your bi-annual pay by 6

- If you are paid annually, divide your annual pay by 12

2. List All Expenses (fixed & variable).

Write down all your household expenses

- Fixed Recurring Expenses - Expenses which repeatedly occur at some regular interval (monthly, quarterly, yearly, etc.), and exist in amounts that are roughly predictable at each occurrence. Examples are rent, mortgage payments, car loan payments, credit card payments, student loan payments, auto insurance, life insurance, medical insurance, electric and gas, water and utilities, mobile phone, cable / satellite television subscriptions.

- Variable Expenses - Expenses which occur at no specific time intervals, and exist in amounts that may be difficult to predict at each occurrence. Some examples are groceries, household items, gifts, personal items, hobby items, entertainment, education, home repairs, car fuel and repairs.

- You should average your fuel bills and telephone bill over the previous twelve months to get a relatively reliable monthly figure.

- Housekeeping is probably the most difficult figure to work out. It is important that you are realistic about what you need to live on. That is one of the reasons for creating the daily spending diary. Don't try to cut down on essentials. If you don't have a clear idea of what you spend on housekeeping, keep a diary of all you spend for a further 30 days to get a better picture.

- Travel expenses - If you have a car or van you should include MOT and repair costs as well as the regular amount of fuel you use. If you don't have a car put down what you regularly spend on rail/bus fares or taxis.

- You also need to make allowances for additional spending during the festive seasons like Christmas so you won't have to use a credit card over that period. Cut your coat according to your size; don't try to outdo your neighbours.

- Saving for emergencies - Even if it is just £1 a week (which is just too ridiculously low) start saving for emergencies now. Create a category for it and allocate money to it as part of your monthly expense.

- If you are putting a percentage of your income aside on a regular basis in any other type of saving scheme, then you might need to consider cancelling that saving until you have managed to reduce your debt to such an extent that you are able to cover your expenses with your income.

3. Compare Income and Expenses.

Now that you have calculated your income and expenses in Steps 1 and 2, compare them. The difference is what is called your Cash Flow or Disposable Income.

Total Income	£ 2525
Minus	
Total Expenses	£2405
Equals **(Cash Flow)**	£ 120

If your total income is larger than your total expenses, then you have a positive Cash Flow. This amount is what you will use towards reaching your short- and long-term goals. On the other hand, if your total expenses are more than your total income, then you are overspending and your debt is increasing monthly. It will be increasingly difficult to reach any of your short- or long-term goals if you continue to increase your total debt every month. Therefore, you need to immediately and carefully adjust your spending.

Whether you are saving money each month or going further into debt, you could probably now manage your money even better than you used to do. **Remember, you can only manage what you can measure**.

4. Set Priorities and Make Changes.

If your cash flow is negative, take heart - at least you can see the situation now in 'black and white' or should I say 'red and white' and you can now tackle the problem from its source.

There are two ways to go about it immediately: You can earn more money or you can spend less - it is as simple as that.

- Decrease your spending and/or
- Increase your income

Unfortunately, it is easier said than done and that's why many people get into debt in the first place by topping up the deficit with money from credit cards and other high interest loans.

Your Spending Plan will help you to focus on areas where you can cut your spending. Obviously you will be looking at luxury items first and those non-essential items that will be easy to eliminate. If you can eliminate your Cash Flow deficit by getting rid of these non-essential items, then you are blessed however it might not be quite that easy for you to reduce your spending enough to turn your Cash Flow positive. If that is the case, then you will have to go back over your Spending Plan again and see the areas where you can cut your spending to try to close the gap between income and expenditure.

Of course you know that you will still continue to pay utility bills, insurance premiums, a mortgage or rent. If you have credit cards, you know that you will have minimum payments to make on those. Also, the monthly payment for your outstanding loans must be made. After these, you now have to draw the line between necessities and luxury; cut off items you can do without – for a little while at least. Remember, the more you can reduce your expenses, the more the cash flow you will have and the sooner you will be debt free."

"Sumptus censum ne superset." (Latin)
"Let not your spending exceed your income." (English)
(Anonymous)

"Remember that the cuts you make in spending are just temporary. Don't' fall into the trap of feeling forever deprived – which can be depressing. When you feel like giving up on reducing your debt, remember that small steps show results cumulatively. If you stop taking those small steps, you will not see the results of all of them. If you stick to it, in a few months you will see what you have accomplished and soon you will have more choices again.

"Once all areas of cost-cutting have been exhausted and your Cash Flow is still negative, then you are left with the only other alternative of increasing your income. This may take a little time; you will need to look at whether you're able to increase your hours of work or possibly even get a second job to bring in enough additional income to cover your expenses.

"One way or another unless this negative cash flow is eliminated you will be destined to continue accumulating debt. The more you do that, the more difficult it will be to bridge the gap between your income and expenses."

"Why don't we just increase our income and not bother with the spending plan?" Desmond asked seeking a way out of the calculation that he knows he will soon be performing.

"I think we should do this Spending Plan stuff, even though it may take a little time. At least to see what we are spending money on" Sally advocated.

"Hear me out first. For some families, it takes about six months to get their Spending Plan balanced out", Craig said.

"This all depends on each family's situation, including how much or what kind of debt they have. On the upside, just like people who begin exercising for the first time tend to see results sooner than the regulars, you may find that your Spending Plan has immediate benefits for you. Therefore, creating it will be time well-spent. Progress and not perfection is what we are striving for here."

"Now to answer your question Desmond: It is not odd that the natural solution to 'money-is-not-enough' seems to be increasing income rather than decreasing spending, and unfortunately some debt counsellors take this albeit backwards approach. If you simply increase your income without a Spending Plan to handle the extra cash properly, the gains tend to slip through the cracks and vanish also. Imagine your financial situation to be a water tank – with leakages draining away your water. Pouring more water will not make the tank full as long as the leakages are not blocked. The more you look at your expenditure, the more shocked you will be when you realise how much money you spend on things that you don't even think about. It is the little bits and pieces of expenditure that accumulate into a bigger debt problem and these are your leakages. I cannot emphasis it enough - no matter how much you earn; you need a Spending Plan."

"If, by some miracle, you find a new way to increase your regular income BEFORE you start decreasing your expenditure, go for it – as long as you realise the need to still create the Spending Plan."

"Thank you for that Craig. Your analogy about the water tank is just spot-on" Sally commented.

"You're welcome."

"Okay Craig. Let's say we've created the Spending Plan ...." Desmond began.

"I hope you're still not trying to dodge the Plan?" Craig asked Desmond, stopping him in midsentence.

"No I'm not; I just need to ask a question. What if we have a **surplus** - I mean positive cash flow?" Desmond asked "Not that I can't think of several things to use the cash for. You know what I'm saying?"

"Ah!" Craig began "That's one of the aims of creating a Spending Plan. You will be able to build a cash cushion for emergencies, apply the cash towards clearing some debt or start your investing with it depending on your strategy.

"Until you have cleared your debt, I will not advise you to consider using the surplus for investing, the reason being that the money you will receive from the investment, less the tax that you will pay on that income, may be less than the amount you will save in interest payments for clearing your debt. Apart from that you cannot afford to risk (not to talk of lose) any money now. Always look for the most benefits for each pound spent and in almost all cases there is no better benefit than clearing the debt that's hanging around your neck. You will even get to sleep better at night.

"Building wealth is something you can look forward to once you have been able to eliminate your debt. With your ability to plan your spending well, you will be able to calculate the ratio of Price-To-Earning and determine whether it is a good investment that you will be able to handle comfortably before you spend your money. You will be able to make all your decisions based on simple steps that will eliminate all the guesswork and ensure that you don't get into financial difficulty again."

"Sometimes you only need to change a few factors in your lives to go from a negative to a positive cash flow and that is what you will be aiming to do as soon as possible. The more of the cash flow surplus you apply to debt the bigger the surplus will become as your individual loans and credit cards become eliminated and the debt-elimination become accelerated over time. Only remember that there is no freedom without sacrifice. We will start dealing with what to do with the surplus from the next session – so just hang on."

"I know you've said a lot today Craig but I still have one more question" Sally said.

"Fire on.", Craig replied.

"What are the effects of **just breaking even**, that is having a cash flow of just above £0?" Sally asked, just wanting to cover all angles.

"At the very beginning, that may not be a bad thing, at least you are not getting deeper into debt but at the same time you are not making any real headway in eliminating your debt either. At that rate, and all things being equal, you will have to wait for each credit card or loan (at least the first one) to run its course before your cash flow can increase. That is a very long road to take to achieve freedom from debt. You will therefore be losing thousands of pounds to your creditors in interest charges. Also if during that time an emergency arises, your Spending Plan will be torn to shreds. Why? You've been 'living on the edge' with your nearly-zero cash flow which means you will have to fall back into debt again. If your cash flow is nearly zero, secure an additional source of income. Do you understand what I'm driving at?"

"I do. Thanks" Sally answered. "That was one of those 'just-in-case' questions."

"I understand" Craig said, getting ready to wind-up for the day.

"Let's just cover all the bases then, shall we?" Desmond said before Craig could say another word. "What if after creating the Spending plan, reducing the expenditure and increasing the income, the cash flow is still negative?"

"That is not the best position to be but all is still not lost" Craig answered. "Just as we have discussed before, what you've described now is a situation of going deeper into debt instead of

79

coming out of it. Therefore, before your creditors start contacting you, contact them first alerting them of your current financial situation. You only need to do this if you are in real financial difficulty but desperate times call for desperate measures. Most lenders would rather work out a repayment plan that you can handle, which could include reducing the interest rate you're paying, than bring in an expensive debt collector. So call them, tell them you have a plan of action - and that you need their help to enable you to pay them back in full. Your Spending Plan will come into play here. I hope your situation won't be like this or you will have lots of phone calls to make."

"And letters to write too" Desmond added.

"This month's exercise is simple but vital" Craig said in conclusion. "You've got to measure what you have first before you can manage them. As I've always told my clients, **'what you cannot measure, you cannot manage'** and it is as simple as that.

"With you two working together on your figures, your first Spending plan should be ready within hours. You can send me a copy if you wish to have another pair of eyes look at it.

"Take note that developing your Spending Plan isn't like *writing in stone*, you can change the Plan anytime; actually you will need to adjust it several times over the next few months. To stay on track, you will need to review your Spending Plan every few months – tweak the categories, cost as well as your spending habits. You will also need to track all your spending at least once every six months – until you are living in the freedom of a debtless life. This requires a lot of self-discipline, but it is mandatory, not optional if you are serious about been totally debt-free.

"One little trick that will help your Spending Plan come together faster is to focus on the rewards – your life goals which you set a few weeks ago. If you are constantly looking at what you have to cut and give up, the very act of creating any spending plan will become rather depressing. Watching your goals slowly but surely become a reality can be very satisfying and provide further motivation to work harder at your next milestone – whatever it may be.

"You have a nice weekend or what's left of it and we shall meet again next month." With that Craig cut the telephone connection leaving the Ellmases to discuss the day's session and begin working on their Spending Plan.

Milestone #2

Save £1000 for Emergencies

Chapter 6

Emergency Fund - Level 1

Just over a week ago Sally suggested the use of a VOIP app (like SKYPE, Zoom, or Teams) for their monthly 'meetings' with Craig. Desmond and Craig decided which app the would use. They talked each other through the already simple set-up process and within 10 minutes of downloading, installation and customisation, Desmond and Craig were already smiling and waving to each other on their computer monitors like two little children.

"This is a good idea Desmond. Now I can see as well as hear you both at the same time. You know I've heard about this technology but I just never bothered to investigate it at all; but here I am using it" Craig began saying after he had adjusted his webcam so the Ellmases could see him well.

"So, are we ready Desmond?" Craig asked.

"Sure"

"Can you hear me Sally?"

"Yes and I can see you too" Sally replied.

"Okay. Now that we are together in sight and sound, let's begin." Craig said.

"Lead the way Craig" Desmond said, encouraging him.

"First of all, I want to congratulate you on the completion of your first or should I say 'trial' Spending Plan that you emailed to me. With that in place we now have something to build on.

"As I went through your Spending Plan, I noticed that you seemed to have forgotten about some items. You did not put anything in the categories for clothes, entertainment and most importantly - the Tithe (or anything to be given to charity). All three are very important and should be included in your Spending Plan.

"No matter how small you want to make it, don't cut clothing off completely as you will need clothes to go to work to be able to make money; not to talk of your fast-growing children. Put in a figure for clothing that shows the cost for the whole household. If you rely on a catalogue for all your clothing (watch how much you are paying them!!), you may want to put the regular monthly payments down for clothing costs.

"Thanks Craig for bringing that up; it was an oversight surely. I have a question though; I understand putting aside some money towards clothing but entertainment .... I don't know. Won't that defeat the whole purpose of debt freedom?" Desmond asked rather more bemused than confused.

"No, it won't. You don't want to become a grouch or a 'Scrooge' while trying to get out of debt. Allow yourselves some breathing space during this period; that is why I want you to set aside some money, no matter how small, for entertainment. Striving to achieve debt freedom is a lot like dieting, if you cut everything out all at once then you are more likely to cheat! Therefore, plan a little for entertainment, but limit the amounts you spend – enjoy yourselves within reason so you don't end up entertaining yourself to the 'poor house'.

The Tithe

"This is a 'biggie' and I'm going to lay it down for you just as it is. I have known you guys to be Christians since our college days and you haven't told me anything has changed so I'm going to go *spiritual* on you.

"I have always wondered why Christians cut the Tithe off at the first sign of trouble or even use it for emergencies. You see, God cannot wait to bless us, but He is waiting to see if we will take Him seriously. As far as He is concerned, He should be first in our lives.

"The Tithe is ten percent (10%) of all our income which we give to God through the local church. Tithe is NOT church taxation or what you are 'helping the church out' with. Tithing unlocks the door of our hearts to be able to enjoy God more fully. That is why tithing is voluntary; God will not punish you for not paying it but you are shutting the windows of heaven against your own finances. Remember God Force One? You are the ones to invite Him into your finances and the main indication of your trust in Him is by paying the Tithe."

"It is only for the present time that we've left the Tithe out, we just think we can catch up later" Sally said, trying to explain.

"I haven't seen anyone who has caught up yet or know if they've caught up. Where will the extra money to 'catch up' come from?" Craig asked. Without waiting for an answer he continued, "Waiting until you have enough money before you can tithe is like saying to a fireplace 'give me heat and I'll give you wood'. You are putting the proverbial cart before the horse."

"Sally, your Spending Plan is more than just a financial document; it is a spiritual document also. The items you have on it show in financial terms, where your heart is spiritually. What you do with your material assets truly reflects the state of your heart spiritually. It shows whether you are living for God or living for yourselves. Tithing is a matter of trust. It is the act of giving back to God the first and the best of our lives in gratitude and thanksgiving for all God has entrusted to us. God needs to be given what's right not what's left - after you've satisfied everybody and everything."

"If we add the Tithe together with clothing and entertainment to our spending plan now, our cash flow will be only about £15 every month" Desmond said after a brief calculation.

"Congratulations!" Craig said excitedly "At least you have positive cash flow. All you need to do now is find ways of increasing it and at the same time you have an opportunity to see Malachi 3 work in your lives as it has done for me. Malachi 3:10 says '**Bring the whole tithe into the storehouse, that there may be food in my house. Test me in this, says the LORD Almighty, and see if I will not throw open the windows of heaven and pour out so much blessing that you will not have room enough for it'.**

"We desperately need the windows of heaven to open wide on us. We will start tithing again from this month" Desmond said in conclusion.

"I'm glad Desmond (and Sally) for your obedience to God's word. God wants to be first in all areas of our lives; if we make Him a priority, He will make us a priority. Also if you obey His principles, you will obtain His promises. I'd better round up on this tithing thing with this A&Q for easy 'digestion':

- **Who should tithe?** All Christians who desire to worship God.

- **What to tithe?** 10% of your increase - to God

- **Where to tithe?** Where you're being fed spiritually – your church

- **Why tithe?** To worship God

- **How to tithe?** By faith, diligently, promptly and cheerfully."

"What about Christian who don't pay Tithe?" Sally just couldn't resist asking. "We have faithfully tithed about until three months ago...."

".... And that was when we kind-of jumped from the 'frying pan into the fire'" Desmond added, finishing the sentence for his wife. "I think with our action, we actually started leaving God out of our financial situation."

"Many churches today faithfully teach on the subject of tithing all over the world. But that said, Christians who don't pay tithe may not have been taught to do it at all or maybe they just lack the right understanding of tithing. Others with the right understanding don't tithe because of unbelief, fear of the future (instead of trust in God), greed or just plain, old selfishness. They believe everything they read in newspapers but question anything that has to do with God and still they expect Him to bless their finances. They sing 'Lord I give You my heart, I give You my soul, *but leave my purse alone ...*'"

"You know what, even those who are not Christians practice the principle of tithing; that is why many of them give to charities and they usually give about 10% and above. They understand that giving is a foundational attitude toward a fuller life. The giver sees the glass as *half full* on the way to becoming *full*. Thus, the givers celebrate each act of giving; they find joy and excitement in it. On the other hand, the people who hold back see life's glass as *half empty*. They hold on to a limited supply and thus overrule the natural order of **giving** *as a* **source** *for* **new supply - from God**. If you use what is in your hand s to do what God wants, your hands will always be full."

89

"Okay 'Pastor Craig' point taken. What's next?" Desmond asked laughing at how serious Craig talked against lack of trust in God.

"Now I will tell you what to do with your £15 cash flow" Craig announced.

"Meaning.... we have NOTHING left after all!!" Sally concluded.

"It isn't that bad, you still have your entertainment allowance." Craig corrected her. "Just hear me out first."

Save £1000 for Emergencies

"Today's session officially starts now." Craig announced.

"It's about time" Desmond joked.

"Very funny. First of all, let me ask you a small question ..." Craig began again.

"Oh-oh, here we go again. Whenever you call anything 'small', it always turns out to be something 'big'. I just know it." Desmond interrupted. "How 'small' a question are we talking about this time?"

"Go on Craig, what is it?" Sally asked curiously, giving her husband the 'this is serious business' look.

"How soon can you raise £1000 without borrowing?"

"What for?" Desmond demanded. "Are you now charging us for your services?"

"Uhmmm ... That's not a bad idea but NO, it is your next Milestone. You need to raise £1000 in reserve for emergencies." Craig informed the Ellmases.

"What!" Desmond started, not quite believing what he just heard. "A whole £1000!! We need money to pay off our debt and you are asking us to save such a large sum!!! By the way, where are we supposed to get it from??? From what we've done so far, we will only have £15 left over each month."

"You are right on track Desmond" Craig replied. "These are just some of the same comments and questions that I have been getting over the years concerning this particular Milestone. You've played your part well - like a pro. Well done.

"Your reaction stems from the age-old question of 'should I save, invest or pay-off my debt?'. As a general rule in the financial world, you will be told is to pay off your debts, such as your personal loans, store cards and credit cards, before you start to save money. I agree with that - bearing in mind that the Emergency Fund is NOT your everyday savings. This is a special kind of saving and also a very important milestone on your journey to financial freedom. Without it you may just be marching-on-the-spot instead of making any progress. You know - like '**activity without productivity**'. I will explain in a minute.

"The £15 cash flow you just mentioned will be going straight toward this £1000 emergency fund and so you only have £985 more to reach the milestone. Any savings you currently have should go into this fund for now. It is easier to use the £1000 you have saved for emergencies than to pay back £1000 that you charged in absolute panic on your credit card."

91

> "Go to the ant, you sluggard; consider her ways, and
> be wise: which having no guide, overseer, or ruler,
> provides her meat in the summer, and gathers her
> food in the harvest."
> Proverbs 6:6-8 (The Bible)

What is an Emergency Fund?

"Before I go on, what do you understand by an Emergency Fund?" Craig asked.

"That's easy. It is the fund you use for any emergency purposes that may crop up" Sally volunteered.

"Well said my friend, thank you. These emergencies may be events such as the loss of a job (or other drops in income), an illness, those high vet bills, an unplanned school trip or a major unexpected expense. The purpose of the fund is to improve your financial security by creating a buffer or safety net of money that can be used to meet emergency expenses as well as reduce (if not totally eliminate) the need to use high interest debt, such as credit cards, as a last resort.

"Note that financial institutions don't carry accounts labelled as emergency funds; it is up to you guys to set up the account and designate it for emergency fund. Make sure this fund is separate from your retirement or investment savings when you start them. Your retirement is still (or should I say 'seems') many years away but an emergency can occur at any minute. You start investing seriously when your family's immediate survival is secured i.e. your debt paid off.

"Your emergency fund must be highly liquid – placed in an account such as current, savings or money market accounts.

This allows quick access to funds, which is vital in real emergency situations. The reason for putting the fund in an account and not under your mattress is just that you won't be tempted to begin using it to pay the pizza delivery guy or gal; also it is not solely for yielding interest either – even though that won't hurt a bit but easy (*and not too easy*) access is the main reason.

"Most financial planners suggest that an emergency fund should contain enough money to cover at least three to six months of living expenses for any unpleasant surprises. To speed up the process of your debt-freedom, we are going to start by building a partial emergency fund which is why we are aiming for £1000 at the moment.

"You will want (and need) to build your emergency fund as quickly as possible. For someone who lives in a rented home and has only a modest amount of debt, an initial emergency fund of £500 may work just fine. If you own a house, a car and other things that can unexpectedly require cash infusions, then your initial emergency fund will need to be bigger - £1000. The key is to build the fund at regular intervals, consistently devoting a certain percentage of each paycheque towards it and, if possible, putting in whatever you can spare on top. This will speed up the process and get you to think about your spending.

What Constitutes an Emergency?

"Here's where it can get a little trickier. You should only use the emergency money for true emergencies: like when your car breaks down, or you lock yourselves out of the house, or your water heater starts to hiss and spit green bile like the demonised girl in the film 'Exorcist'. Covering regular purchases like clothes and food do not count, even if you have used your credit card to buy them.

"The fact that the three-piece-suit which 'has your name written all over it' at your favourite Department store is only on sale today does not constitute an emergency. You have other clothes to wear; if you want this suit, wait and save for it.

"The £250 dress chosen for your cousin's sudden wedding next Thursday (after a three-week, whirlwind romance with his new girlfriend) is NOT an emergency. Someone else's lack of planning should not become an emergency on your part. Think about this, if you spend your emergency fund on the quick wedding and your car breaks down on your way back home; what do you do? You will be forced to borrow (on credit card) for the repairs won't you? You go back to the same old borrowing habit again.

"Sally, please don't let that man called Desmond talk you into buying the new 65-inch 8K-TV now. If the current TV is still working, you don't need to go into debt to get a new one.

"Craaaiiiig! I thought you are my friend!!" interjected Desmond.

"I am, believe me, I am; but this is war on debt and we must win - by all means. The same thing goes for all other household goods as well - essential or luxury items. You should use the old World War II saying which goes like this: **'Use it up, Wear it out; Make it do, or Do without'**. Do whatever is necessary to survive without going into debt. Don't get me wrong, the time is coming when you will be able to afford three each of such items (at once if you so wish) without borrowing.

"It is true that you would save money if you used your emergency fund to eliminate credit card debt or pay off loans but what happens when an emergency occurs soon after that.

94

You are forced to go and borrow again since you have no cash cushion to fall back on. The purpose of the fund is to prevent you from having to use your credit card for paying for the ugly things that life might throw at you. With a proper emergency fund, you will not need your credit card to float you when something goes wrong.

"You need to view your emergency fund not as a luxury but as a necessity like the life insurance policy that we talked about several weeks ago. Once you have it, guard it very carefully. It's not a piggy bank or pocket money so you shouldn't be dipping into it for incidental expenses. Use it only in the event of an emergency, and hope that an emergency never happens.

"Remember, once that money is spent – on a real emergency, you need to replace it quickly. By the time you have the complete £1000, you would have inculcated the habit of saving into your lifestyles but watch out because the time it takes to replace varies and it depends on your Spending Plan at that time. Start now and save whatever you can, even if it isn't much. Someday, when you need the money, you'll be glad you had the fund."

Ways to Build Up the Emergency Fund

"How much savings do you have at present for anything – emergencies or not?" Craig asked.

"We have about £380 in a savings account that we haven't dipped into yet" Sally replied.

"That's quite good. If you add that to the £15 cash flow you have coming in at the end of this month, you will have £395 leaving you with only £605 to go. This is looking really good but there are other things you can do to speed up the accumulation of the remaining amount. I will give you a few suggestions that may help you along the way:

1. Go through your house and gather ALL the items you have that are unwanted, unused and sellable. Turn them to cash on EBay or at car-boot sales in town. I know of a lady who made over £2000 in a ten-month period selling her old (but still in very good condition) clothes on EBay. It usually takes a little more effort to sell stuff than it takes to lay the credit card on the counter for buying. According to the lady in question, de-cluttering her wardrobe was a big job, but she painstakingly photographed all the clothes, uploaded the pictures on to EBay and the rest is history. Making money online is now a part of her regular income-generating strategy.

2. Open a high-yield online savings account with as little as one pound and automate the deposit of your monthly (positive) cash flow into it.

3. Empty your pocket change into a jar every night. Bring the content of your coin jar to the bank every month for deposit. Those coins can really add up.

4. Don't touch, but divert any raise or bonus you get (if its not part of your Spending Plan already) straight into the emergency fund.

5. Evaluate your cable/satellite TV package. Do you really need 400-plus channels? Do you have time to watch those movie or sports channels you're paying a premium price for? You can always rent movies when you want to watch any particular one. Switch to basic cable and save some money each month.

6. Visit the library rather than your local bookstore. Besides books, you can borrow movies, music CDs and even exercise videos from the library. Check the selection available at your local library and keep yourself entertained for free.

7. Cancel subscriptions to magazines and newspapers you haven't been reading. Or see if the publication has an online version you can access for free or less than a printed copy.

8. Downgrade your telephone service. Call waiting and call-redirection which can be very costly.

9. Consider switching your land line phone service to an internet (voice over IP or VOIP) service - if you use the internet for very long periods during the day.

10. Bring your own lunch to the office. Research has shown that we spend an average of £4.40 on lunch each working day which adds up to £1, 050 a year. Thus workers shell out £42,000 on sandwiches and snacks in their lifetime.

11. Drink water rather than soft drink when you're dining out.

12. Switch to store-brand food item.

13. Stock up on non-perishable shopping items when they are on sale.

14. Do all your weekly shopping in one trip. You will save time, energy and fuel too.

15. Slow down on fast food for a while. The cumulative amount you spend in those fast-food joints can be staggering.

16. Tutor a young student in a subject you know if you can create the time.

17. Get a part-time job at your favourite store. If you are going to be there, you might as well make some money while enjoying the atmosphere.

18. Work a few extra hours at your day job if possible.

19. Shop around to ensure all your financial accounts do not charge you extraneous fees.

20. Always know how much you have in the bank so your accounts will never be overdrawn or be charged a fee.

21. Use public transportation rather than driving when possible and if it will save you money.

22. Save on fuel by not driving faster than 65 miles per hour.
23. Delay vacations until your emergency fund is complete.
24. Call your insurance provider and ask for an updated quote to see if you get a reduction in your premium.
25. Shop around for a new insurance provider.
26. Negotiate in any retail environment. The more you try, the less you'll spend (and the more you can save for emergencies).
27. Don't be an early adopter of new technology. Wait until the initial high price has been reduced before joining in the technology.
28. Cancel your gym membership. Find other cheaper and fun ways to exercise.
29. Consider adopting a frugal philosophy, at least until the emergency fund is in place and you are out of debt.
30. While paying attention to small, repetitive expenses, **don't ignore larger items** like your car, house, and wedding. With smart choices on big-ticket items, you could fully fund an emergency account with the savings.

"During this initial stage of raising funds for emergencies, you will be making a lot of sacrifices. Just be aware that a slight decrease in quality of life in the short term will likely outweigh long-term financial devastation when a future emergency arises.

"While you are making sacrifices and focusing on becoming debt-free don't be surprised if your friends ridicule you for what you are doing. It happened to me. My friends and colleagues made fun of my new frugal lifestyle but I did not let that deter me from reaching for my debt freedom goal. They laughed at how they thought I had no more burning urges to buy new clothes, cars, furniture and so on unless I had saved up the cash first. (The temptations were still there, I just resisted them successfully). I have since helped many of those same people create their Spending Plans amongst other things after they began to see the fruits of my 'labour'.

"Your debt-free strategy will, apart from planning and determination, take creativity and some hard work. But If I could do it alone, you two can encourage each other and reach your financial goals. Don't get me wrong, you may still hang out with your friends you just won't do the expensive forms of entertainment with them anymore."

"That's going to be tough" Desmond moaned "I'm missing my golf buddies already. Now you have to add this....?"

"We are still going to see our friends; you just won't be spending freely like you used to do before" Sally said comforting her husband while poking fun at him.

"Me?" Desmond objected before he could stop himself. Then he remembered how he always tried to be the 'big guy' during those frequent 'let's do lunch' events with his friends.

> "If you do what you OUGHT to do, when you OUGHT to do it, the day will come when you will be able to do what you WANT to do when you WANT to do it."
> - Zig Ziglar

"Relax my friends. This may be a good time to ask you to begin to think of how you will be celebrating your debt freedom even when you still have (and only have) your mortgage left to pay off.

"Now we're talking" Desmond said, grateful to Craig for changing the subject quickly.

"You see at that time you would have scraped and sacrificed for months or even years. It will then be time to treat yourselves to whatever you fancy or maybe just kick back for a week on a Cruise of your choice. Find what fits your liking and your spending plan. Have fun, reap the deserved rewards of your hard work, and pay for it all in cash!

"You may even have a Credit card/Loan shredding party with your close friends – make sure you invite me. This is a great way to celebrate with friends and do a little financial evangelising at the same time. At least now your friends will see the result of all the cutting-back which you've been doing for many months. Just make sure you do everything within reason."

"Thanks Craig I'll take care of that when the time comes" Sally assured him.

"Remember you have to be debt-free before you can have a debt-free party!"

Milestone #3

Pay Off Credit Cards

Chapter 7

Pay Off Credit Cards

As soon as Sally's face showed up on his monitor, Craig greeted her saying "Hi Sally, how are things going with you guys?"

"We are fine. Thanks Craig, for agreeing to our request of having this session today instead of two weeks ago. I just wanted to make sure we got a bit more of the emergency fund before we continue to the next stage. I never thought getting rid of some of those seemingly 'sentimental' items could bring so much relief and cash! We got just under £300 from the car boot sale last week Sunday - £293 to be exact. Now I have space in the house that I never knew existed. We have been able to get £988 of the £1000 emergency fund now. We diverted Desmond's backdated bonus that he received from his company this quarter, the few pounds from three of our old savings accounts (one of which is where we are saving the emergency fund at the moment) together with the proceeds from the car-boot sale."

"Good for you Sally. You guys are blessed to have been able to get this in so short a time. You seem to have money lying all around your home that you didn't know about until now.

"You are correct" Sally agreed. "I still find it hard to believe that in only six weeks we have almost £1000!"

"For most people, it will take a lot longer than that. They have to first of all, take time and a lot more effort to make their expenditure lower than their income; to enable them to have some positive cash flow; and then begin to build that excess cash into the initial emergency fund.

"Try and complete the £1000 as soon as possible so you will know that you have actually reached the second milestone. De-clutter the house more and you will find more 'hidden money'. If you want to venture into online selling, there are lots of websites like EBay that you can register with. You will need the funds even after you become completely debt free."

Breaking Card Habits

"Craig, from the list you gave us, getting rid of credit card debts is supposed to be the next milestone. Why are we separating credit cards from other debts?" Sally asked itching to begin the day's session.

"Habits sister, habits" Craig replied. "By the way, where's Des?"

"I'm right here Craig" Desmond replied bending down beside Sally so Craig could see his face through the webcam "I have been thinking about the same question; can you explain the logic behind this thinking to us?"

"Yes, no problem. You would have noticed in my list that I divided the whole Journey to Financial Freedom into simple goals that I call **Milestones**. These milestones are the little victories that we will aim for, achieve (and celebrate) along the way. A victory is more than merely winning a battle; it is more like changing a habit, lifestyle, culture and ultimately changing your family tree financially. That is, what has hurt you both until now will not even be experienced by your children (and grandchildren) because you changed your habits and passed the new habits on to them."

How Credit Cards Work – *Against You*

"Credit cards can be compared to drugs - they offer short-term pleasure (in the form of easy money or convenience) and long-term pain. They give the illusion of you having more money than you actually do; but then you live with even less money because each month a portion of your income is being siphoned away to pay past credit card debt.

"On face value, credit cards are great! Picture this: You can walk into any store and buy some expensive clothes or gadgets, whip out your card, sign your name or enter your PIN (Personal Identification Number), and walk out without spending any money! Or so you think. What could be better? Thirty days later though, the bill comes in the mail asking you to pay only 2% of all that you owe. That's chicken change; you pay it and continue spending. As time goes on, however, the balance of that card gets bigger and bigger – even though you are making the minimum monthly payments!

"Before you know it, you owe thousands of pounds on the card, your minimum monthly payment has risen to an unmanageable amount, and the credit card company starts calling you almost daily about paying your bill while adding late payment fees (and reminder charges) to your account. The once-beautiful, precious, platinum, gold or black, can't-leave-home-without-it credit card has just become a nightmare."

"We've been there" Desmond said.

"We're still there" Sally corrected.

"Credit card companies work to make sure that you stay in debt or else they will soon go out of business which is something THEY are not prepared to do at all. It is as simple as that. As long as you are in debt to them, they are making money – and the more debt you have, the more money they make. Why do you think they make the minimum monthly payments so small?

"To make sure people can afford it" Desmond blurted out unsure of himself or his answer.

"Their purpose is to get you hooked and then bleed you dry – one drop (or is it one pound or dollar) at a time; ultimately draining you of your future health and wealth. The typical minimum monthly payments used to be 10% of your balance several years ago, but gradually they've been reduced to 5% and then 3% and now even 2%. Is it because they like you? NO!!! With interest adding around 1.5% a month to your balance, if you're only paying 2% a month then you don't need a degree in accounting to work out that you'll only pay off a tiny amount each time – if you only pay the minimum they require of you.

"Credit card companies are not on your side at all. Sure, they make it easy for you to buy that new living room furniture or the latest technological gadget your heart is so set on. If you want that fancy exercise equipment that was 'made just for you', they will help you get it. Only understand that they will want you to pay for the privilege and convenience, with interest and for as long as possible – the rest of your life if you choose. The length of time it takes to clear credit card debts when paying only the minimum required each month is shocking – so is the amount paid during that time. It can take 40 years or more to clear a card with balance of a few thousand pounds – if you only pay the minimum required monthly.

"To look like the good guys (and because they are forced to do so by the law), credit card companies now put warnings on their statements indicating how paying only the minimum will affect the length of time it will take you to clear your debt but many people still go from month to month making just the minimum payments. They know many people won't heed the warning at the bottom of the paper and they are right.

> **"Life was a lot simpler when what we honoured was father and mother rather than all major credit cards."**
>
> - Robert Orben

"While we are getting warm on this topic, let me tell you about a sneaky, little trick that credit card companies used for many years (before government intervention) to distribute any money you pay them towards whatever your credit card balance was. They called it Negative Payment Hierarchy."

"What's that?" Desmond asked.

"I know hearing the word 'negative' will cause alarm bells to start ringing, it was really something they didn't like to talk about because it was a scary, little, monster of a trick. Negative Payment Hierarchy is when the credit card payments you make are distributed in such a way that they go towards paying off your cheapest debts first.

"You see, your credit card balance may be a mixture of purchases, balance transfers from a previous credit card and some unfortunate cash withdrawals (ouch!). You should know that different types of credit card debts attract different interest rates; those nasty cash withdrawals usually have the highest rates while balance transfers often the lowest.

"To clear your balance as fast as possible, you would hope that the debt with the highest interest rate is paid off first when you make your monthly payments - but that was not what happened back then. Instead, the debt with the lowest interest rate was paid off first - leaving you unable to clear the most expensive parts of your balance without paying off everything in one go!

"So your cash withdrawals, which are your most expensive debts, would not be paid off until you have completely cleared your purchase balance and your balance transfer - leaving you with a much larger interest bill than you would have expected. Do you get the picture now?"

"Yeeesss! No wonder our balances don't seem to be decreasing as fast as they should even though we pay more than the minimum sometimes!" Sally exclaimed.

Even though these companies have been mandated to use your payments to pay off the items with the highest interest rates first, that does not mean they have become your friends", Craig cautioned. "Why play with snakes when you know all they are going to do is bite you?"

"Well I guess the fault is ours anyway. We've used the credit cards to withdraw cash as if they were debit cards" Desmond confessed.

"What were the emergencies?" Craig asked.

"None comes to mind right now really. I think we just needed cash during those times" Sally said keeping the confessing going.

"Uhmmmm...", Craig said shaking his head. "Not your most brilliant moves to date and you had to pay for the privilege of just taking the cash out in form of withdrawal fee."

"We know that now" Desmond admitted with huge sigh of regret about his cash-withdrawing blunders. "Just don't rub it in – the truth is painful enough."

"Don't worry, all that will be reversed soon; so that more of your hard-earned money will be used for your own good rather than throwing it toward interest payments." Craig said "What we need to start doing now is to pay off the credit cards one after the other because your cash withdrawals are now costing you lots of money in interest."

"Why can't we just consolidate the cards into a loan or move them into a new one with 0% interest for up to 15 months thus paying everything all at once instead of paying them off one at a time" Desmond asked, curious of what Craig is trying to accomplish.

"Good question."

Craig thought for a minute then he asked the Ellmases a question saying "Desmond, Sally, when was the last time that either of you went for a month without using a credit card?"

Desmond responded without much of thought "I can't tell. To be candid, I don't think I have ever stopped using the credit cards since I got my first one and that was since our school days!!"

"The same goes for me too. I have never really given my credit card usage much of a thought." Sally called out from behind her husband.

"It's about time you both left that 'can't-live-without-my-credit-card' club" Craig said to them. "We have established previously that in order for you to dig yourselves out of this debt-hole, you must stop incurring more debt; right?"

"Right"

"With the consolidation of your credit cards into a loan comes, lower monthly payments on the loan, longer payment time and the availability of 'newly-cleaned, zero-balance' credit cards waiting to be used. Please take this from me; whenever money is readily and easily available, people tend to behave irresponsibly – it is just human nature of the 21st century. By the way, you must keep in mind that using a loan to pay off your credit card debt is not reducing your debt; instead, you are only reshuffling the debt in a manner that you think will makes it easier to manage.

"There's the story of a 21-year old computer studies student who thought it would be great fun to use his new shiny credit card to gamble on the internet, until he reached his £1,000 credit limit. Instead of him to knuckle down and repay the cash, he decided to blame his card issuer. His argument was that the card issuer had tempted him into a vice with its generous credit limit. He then, unashamedly, demanded that the card issuer pay his gambling debts for him. His request was rightly turned down. Now, who wants to tell me that if this guy gets another £1000 he will not do the same thing again? It is a matter of habits.

"It has been a habit for you two to continually use your credit cards monthly. Consolidating your credit card balances into a low-interest loan (as good as it may seem) will not suddenly make you stop using the cards. Instead, you need to cultivate a new habit of NOT using the credit cards – full stop! Use your debit card or raw use cash - at least you know you can only spend the money that you have in your pocket, purse or wallet."

"In the same vein, I do not recommend that you remortgage your home or use any line of credit to pay off credit cards. Paying off credit card debt with a home equity line of credit has been a popular move in recent years, as property values soared and mortgage rates hovered near historic lows. But when property prices stall or start to slip, extracting more cash will become a very risky venture indeed. In addition, people who have racked up big balances will soon start to see the terrible 'side' effects of their actions especially when they decide to sell up and move, they may (and most likely will) find that they owe more on the house than the sale price, and that's not going to be funny at all."

While Sally was trying to jot down the key points of the meeting session for review later, Desmond asked "What if we can pay off what we've used on the credit cards at the end of each month?"

"Even if you can pay it off at the end of the month still don't use the credit cards until you have mastery over your credit card usage. Credit cards are not for the undisciplined. It is generally known that you spend about 13% less when you use cold-hard cash. The result will be that you will become debt-free sooner rather than later. Paying with cash makes many people think more carefully about how much they're spending. Parting with a crisp ten-pound note is often more painful than entering a PIN number - so you might be less inclined to fling money around anyhow."

"But we'll be missing out on the rewards some credit cards offer such as cash-back, air miles and holiday discount offers." Desmond observed.

"No you won't. You'll actually be saving yourself a lot of money. You shouldn't be using credit cards for reward or cash-back. If you do use the cards on the other hand, the interest you'll be charged is most likely to far outweigh the benefits you are gunning for.

111

"Do you really know why the credit card companies and stores introduced loyalty point and cash-back schemes?" Craig asked. He then continued without waiting for an answer "The whole idea is to take your eyes away from what you're spending on to the points or cash-back. It is to make you focus more on the points you think you are gaining than on your hard-earned cash that you are actually losing to them in interest – your future wealth.

"Can you even remember how many times you have bought something that you otherwise wouldn't if not for your credit card?" Craig asked his friends again.

"Honestly speaking, I will say countless times" Desmond responded without any hesitation while Sally only nodded her head in agreement beside him.

"I will say it again; credit cards are not for the undisciplined but that's exactly what those companies don't want you to know. They portray the cards as being for the elite saying 'WHAT'S IN YOUR WALLET?' as if they are status symbols or a necessity for people of the in-crowd. What's in your wallet, if used in a careless manner, can hinder your family's freedom financially.

"Please remember that each time you use your precious credit cards, the money you're spending isn't necessarily yours – it is borrowed money. If you really want to take control of your finances use cash – for the time being at least." Craig said putting the issue to rest.

Snowballing Your Credit Card Debt

"So how do you suggest we pay off the cards we have now?" Sally asked to which Craig replied "There are several ways of paying off credit card debt but one of the most effective methods is what is referred to as 'snowballing'."

"Basically you focus on one card at a time, paying each one off as you go along. As your debts decrease, the amount of money you have to attack the cards increases. Your payments snowball until all of your debt is paid off completely.

1. Make a list of all your credit card debts starting with the one with the smallest balance. Don't look at the interest rate at this time. The only time the interest rate should come into play is if you have two balances that are very close.

2. Focus on paying off the credit card with the smallest balance first by applying all your free cash to that card. You need to get really crazy but focused, and take every extra few pounds you have and pay them on this one card. Don't keep the money away until the end of the month because by that time, that money might not be around – if yiu know what I mean. By the end of next month, your statement for that card will start looking really weird. It'll have a whole bunch of credits on it, instead of the usual interest charges and fees! Since this credit card balance is the smallest, just a few months from now, it'll be gone completely.

3. Once the first card is paid off, you use the money you were paying on that card and begin applying that to the balance of the next highest credit card balance. Pay the second card off and keep doing it with the third, fourth, etc. All the while, you make a fixed amount, which is at least the minimum monthly payment for this month, to the other cards that you are not currently focusing on."

"Wait a minute Craig, why are we paying off the smallest balance instead of the card with the highest interest rate?

Won't we be losing money on interest that way?" Desmond asked.

"Your questions are valid and vital" Craig answered. "Many years ago, I would have recommended that route but I won't do that these days; at least not with you. The reason being that many people lack willpower in financial matters; which is often the reason for their having credit card debts in the first place. So I have chosen a method that can motivate them in the rapid payment of those debts.

"Focusing on one credit card at a time allows you to feel a sense of accomplishment when you finally pay it off. With the smallest balance, you will get the fastest result. That will keep you interested in paying off your debt entirely when you begin to see results. You can even have fun with it by challenging yourselves to see how quickly you can pay any particular credit card off.

"That apart, you need to ask yourself this question 'am I aiming to get out of debt as fast as I can or am I just trying to save on interest?'. Getting rid of your credit card balances one at a time and as quickly as possible, increases your disposable income (cash flow) which in turn takes you closer to debt-freedom when you can start to make money from your money."

Minimum Monthly Payment vs Fixed Monthly Payment

"If I may ask, how many credit cards do you have?"

"Four, from next week onward" Sally answered. "We did balance transfer from two cards into one with lower interest rate and we will be cancelling those two cards with the next two weeks when all the transfers would have been completed."

"Before we go on Craig, when you were talking about 'snowballing' I noticed you said we should be making FIXED monthly payments on all other cards while focusing on the one with smallest balance. Why are we not just paying the MINIMUM that is required of us at least for now?" Desmond asked with genuine interest.

"Ah! That's the point I'm getting to. I'm surprised you caught that. What have you been eating?" Craig teased.

"Oh come off it. I listen to everything you say – for the moment at least." Desmond retorted.

"I will try and be very conservative with the example that I'm going to give you here; I will also assume that the absolute minimum payment allowed is even £10 instead of the usual £5[3] which will make the payment period longer.

"If you have a credit card with a balance of £1,000 at 18% interest, it will take you 153 months (which is 12 years and 9 months) to pay it off assuming you only make the minimum payment. That is not to even mention the £1,115.33 you will pay in interest on the original £1,000 you borrowed.

---

[3]. https://moneyfacts.co.uk/credit-cards/guides/what-is-a-minimum-payment-on-a-credit-card/#:~:text=The%20minimum%20payment%20on%20your%20credit%20card%20is,of%20the%20annual%20fee%20if%20there%20is%20one

PAYMENT SCHEDULE

Month	Minimum Payment	Interest Paid	Principal Paid	Remaining Balance
1	£25.00	£15.00	£10.00	£990.00
2	£24.75	£14.85	£9.90	£980.10
3	£24.55	£14.70	£9.80	£970.30
4	£24.26	£14.55	£9.70	£960.60
5	£24.01	£14.41	£9.61	£950.99
||	||	||	||	||
||	||	||	||	||
148	£10.00	£0.82	£9.18	£45.16
149	£10.00	£0.68	£9.32	£35.84
150	£10.00	£0.54	£9.46	£26.68
151	£10.00	£0.40	£9.60	£16.77
152	£10.00	£0.25	£9.75	£7.02
153	£10.00	£0.11	£9.90	£0.00

"The minimum payment on credit card debt is calculated as a percentage of your current balance. The minimum payment drops as your balance is paid, and thanks to the magic of compounding interest working against you this time, you'll end up paying for a long, long time.

"If you fix the minimum payment yourself to that first amount of £25 and you pay that same amount onwards, here is what the payment schedule will be like:

PAYMENT SCHEDULE

Month	Payment	Interest Paid	Principal Paid	Remaining Balance
1	£25.00	£15.00	£10.00	£990.00
2	£25.00	£15.59	£10.16	£979.84
3	£25.00	£15.43	£10.32	£969.53
4	£25.00	£15.27	£10.48	£959.05
5	£25.00	£15.10	£10.65	£948.40
| |	| |	| |	| |	| |
| |	| |	| |	| |	| |
57	£25.00	£1.64	£23.36	£85.64
58	£25.00	£1.28	£23.72	£61.92

59	£25.00	£0.93	£24.07	£37.85
60	£25.00	£0.57	£24.43	£13.42
61	£25.00	£0.20	£24.80	£0.00

"It will take you 61 months (that is 5 years and 1 month) to be rid of your debt. In that time, you will pay only £538.42 in interest!

"Now see what happens if you get radical and add an extra £5 a month to your payment. You can cut the time further down to 47 months (3 years and 11months) and £396.47 in interest as shown below:

PAYMENT SCHEDULE

Month	Payment	Interest Paid	Principal Paid	Remaining Balance
1	£30.00	£15.00	£15.00	£985.00
2	£30.00	£14.78	£15.22	£969.78
3	£30.00	£14.55	£15.45	£954.32
4	£30.00	£14.31	£15.69	£938.64
5	£30.00	£14.02	£15.92	£922.72
||	||	||	||	||

42	£30.00	£2.38	£27.62	£131.15
43	£30.00	£1.97	£28.03	£103.12
44	£30.00	£1.55	£28.45	£74.67
45	£30.00	£1.12	£28.88	£45.79
46	£30.00	£0.69	£29.31	£16.47
47	£30.00	£0.25	£29.75	£0.00

"Depending on how much you pay on your credit cards monthly; you can drastically reduce the time it takes you to pay them off. This is one of the reasons I like the 'snowballing' method.

Credit Card Payment Comparison For £1000 at 18%		
Monthly Payment	Total Interest (approx.)	Time To Repay Debt (approx.)
Minimum (3% or £5)	£1308	18years 6months
Minimum (3% or £10)	£1115	12years 9months
£25.75/month	£511	4years 11months

£30.75/month	£382	3years 9months
£40/month	£262	2years 8months
£50/month	£200	2years
£60/month	£160	1year 8months
£70/month	£134	1year 3months
£80/month	£116	1year 2months

"This illustration above should show you just how long it's going to take you to clear your credit card balance. I'm not asking you put in a lot of funds into all your cards now; what I'm saying is if you can afford to pay the minimum this month, you can afford to pay the same amount next month and other months thereafter. It is the speed of becoming debt-free that I'm interested in. So, wake up, face reality, stop paying the bare minimum and start clearing this punitive form of debt.

"This is one card game you can't afford to play by the rules. Make your own rules; stop using the cards, pay more than the minimum, more than once a month, pay it off completely, cut the card, cancel the account."

Milestone #4

Increase Emergencies Fund to One Month's Living Expenses

Chapter 8

Emergency Fund – Level 2

A few months have passed since Craig set the Ellmases on a warpath against their credit card debt. He has been talking to them from time to time; but this weekend, they were paying him a long-overdue visit.

Athletics has always been a passion of Sally's. Since her primary school days, she had participated in several events including 400 meters and long-jump at district, county and national levels. She was also a champion athlete in her university days; it was during one of those competitions that Desmond, a spectator, first noticed her. So when Craig invited the Ellmases to Birmingham for the weekend and informed them that he had secured tickets for the indoor athletics event taking place at the Indoor Arena, the decision to say 'yes' was quick.

Desmond and Sally arrived on Friday evening as planned. They had dinner with Craig and Michael Gray another old friend from their *alma mater*. Michael worked at the Arena in Birmingham and promised to give them a tour of the centre before the start of the athletics programme on Saturday morning.

Increase Emergency Fund to One Month's Living Expenses

Early the next day, in accordance with previous arrangement, the Ellmases sat with Craig at the dining table for the next step or milestone on their journey to financial freedom.

"As you were saying yesterday Sally, you are beginning to feel free from debt. I know the feeling; it is a good one which should spur you to increase your speed of (and not to become complacent with) getting debt free. Don't even try to relax too much until all debts are paid off completely – including the mortgage."

"Wow" Desmond exclaimed "That will take a long time."

"Not as long as you think if you attack it seriously. We will cross that bridge when we get to it."

"What's for today?" Sally asked.

"This is one of the easiest milestones to reach if your financials habits have truly changed."

"You'd better believe it that they have ..." Desmond started.

"... Or we won't be comfortable facing you now - after all you've shown us" Sally said, somehow completing Desmond's sentence.

"I'm glad to hear that" Craig said. "Now that you have paid off all your credit cards we can safely move to the next milestone – which is ..."

At that moment, the doorbell rang and Craig excused himself as he stood up to answer the door.

It was Michael Gray who wanted to spend some time with his old friends as well as introduce his wife to them before taking them to the NEC Arena.

"Good morning my people!" he said loudly spreading his arms wide as soon as he saw the Ellmases. "I brought someone here to meet you". He then stepped aside to allow a lady with the attire of a Greek temple dancer to fully enter the room.

"This is my wife, Agatha ... and yes she's Greek" Michael said as Desmond stood up. "Our neighbours got to know that this morning too."

"This is Sally Ellmas and her husband Desmond of whom you've heard so much."

"Hi Sally. Hi Desmond. It is nice to *finally* meet you both" Agatha said shaking hands with the Ellmases. "I'm supporting Greece with a few friends today at the Indoor Athletics event we are attending later - thus the costume."

"And I'm supporting Australia" Craig said as he stood with the others.

"You don't say!!" Desmond responded in mock surprise and to the amusement of all the others.

"Ah Milestone Number Four!" Michael said drawing everyone's attention when he saw Craig's notes on the dining table.

"Leave my notes alone Mike" Craig said snatching the papers from him.

"We went through this milestone over two years ago" Michael said turning to the Ellmases. "You are looking at a debt-free couple except for the mortgage which we are working toward paying off completely sooner than the lenders would wish."

"You know we had to downsize our house to get to this stage?" Agatha said to Sally. "Craig helped us to realise that it was actually our very big mortgage on a very big property that was ruining us financially. Instead of remortgaging for a longer period to lower the monthly payment, we sold the property and bought a good-sized, but financially convenient house … and here we are."

"We are no longer 'house poor' as Craig would put it" Michael added as he headed for the kitchen.

"Alright but this morning is not about you two" Craig said as he motioned the Ellmases to the dining table again.

"May I sit with you while you go through the session?" Agatha asked Craig. "I promise to be quiet."

"No problem Agatha."

"As I was saying before I was interrupted by Mr & Mrs Gray" Craig began again, raising his voice slightly so Michael could hear in the kitchen.

"I heard that" Michael responded making everyone to burst into laughter.

"Now that you've finished paying off your credit cards, your next milestone will be …"

"Craig you're doing it again" Agatha interrupted.

"Doing what again?" Craig asked "I thought you said you'll be quiet?"

"I know and I'm sorry but you're leaving something out in this 'card' business just as you did with us, remember?"

"Remember what?"

"You talked about credit cards but you've left out store cards" Agatha reminded him.

"Have I? Craig asked.

"Yes!" everyone chorused including Michael who was coming out of the kitchen with 5 glasses of orange juice on a tray.

"Oh, I'm sorry. I just assumed that a card is a card – credit card or store card. When I talk about credit cards, store cards are also included.

"Store cards work in the same way as credit cards in that you use the card to make purchases in that store instead of cash and you can then make repayments on the amount that you owe either in one go or in monthly instalments.

"In order to try and tempt you, most stores will offer a massive discount on the purchase that you are making at that time you are in the store simply for making an application for the store card. Many people take up these offers right there and then because of the discounts. Taking into consideration that store card interest rates are higher than credit card rates, people seem to be genuinely ignorant about the rates they are signing up to when they take out a store card.

"There is one major disadvantage with the store cards in comparison with credit cards. They can only be used in certain shops or chains, which will really limit your choice when making purchases. The other disadvantage is the extortionate rate of interest that you will pay if you spread your repayments. Once you've paid off these cards, cut them up, close the accounts and just get them out of your lives.

"Is that okay now, Agatha? Craig asked in conclusion.

127

"Yes that's fine; thank you Craig", Agatha replied.

"You are welcome. Now let's move on", Craig said, turning back to the Ellmases.

"After paying off all your credit and store cards and also closing the accounts (leaving no room for temptation), your next milestone is to increase your Emergency Fund to one month's living expenses. This one is simple to reach. Since you already have a Spending Plan, you know exactly how much your one-month's living expenses is. Apart from that, you now have the saving habit. All the cash flow you've been using to pay off your credit (and store) cards will now go into the Emergency Fund. You will reach this goal in a few months."

"Two months actually" Desmond said looking as their spending plan in the papers in his hands.

"That's good; that's very good" Craig said nodding his head and smiling; obviously enjoying this journey to financial freedom as much as the Ellmases are doing.

"Craig, you told us that the ultimate goal for emergency funds is 3-to-6 months of living expenses, since this milestone is so easy to reach, why don't we just do it all at once and then start paying off debt?" Sally asked even though she could almost guess what Craig might say in reply.

"I have been trying, for years, to reconcile between two opposing opinions of having an Emergency Fund in place first and paying off your debt first. However, splitting the emergency fund (and the debts) into distinctive levels seem to have worked well for me so far" Craig replied.

"It worked for us. It helped us to first change our financial habits, then have an emergency fund saved and later pay off our debt" Michael said in agreement.

"That's it folks. Just as simple as I said it will be" Craig said, picking up his notes from the table. "Does anyone have comments or questions?"

"Yes, I have one" Sally responded. "We will obviously reach the fourth milestone in the next two months. Can you take us through the fifth milestone while we are here this weekend?"

"That won't be a problem ..." Craig started to say.

"You will have to postpone that till later if you want to go on the tour of the Arena and still make start of the athletics this morning" Michael jumped in.

"That's true. We'll do it tomorrow since you're not going back to London till Monday" Craig said as he pushed back his chair.

With that, the five of them stood up to begin making their way to the Indoor Arena.

Milestone #5

Pay Off Consumer Debt

Chapter 9

Pay Off Consumer Debt

The church that the Ellmases attended with Craig was as lively as they come. The friendliness of the congregation, beginning with the ushers at the door to the members sitting in the pews and lastly the message for the day got to Sally in particular that it took her a while to stop commenting about everything.

Desmond, on the other hand, was more interested in the music. He was, however, more than satisfied with the very high standard of the worship leaders and the musicians by the time the service was over.

After the church service, Craig took the Desmond and Sally to the Grays' residence where Agatha had prepared lunch for them. Sally and Agatha had time, after lunch, to talk about their feelings about debt freedom and their husbands amongst other things while the men talked about football, old cowboy movies and cars.

The Ellmases returned to Craig's house about 6.30pm and went to have a little rest before having their session with Craig in the evening. Thankfully, the following day, Monday, was a public-holiday, making the weekend a little longer.

Sally took a little time to speak to her daughters who were spending the weekend with Desmond's parents. At the appointed time, the three of them gathered again at the dining table for the fifth milestone to financial freedom.

"I have dealt with people, who think that lenders are to blame for their debt problems and not their own financial indiscretions" Craig began. "These financial institutions are businesses and they are just providing a service from which they hope to make a profit. Even though their profit, gotten mostly through fees and charges, are a lot of the time quite unreasonable but they will never force you or anybody else to borrow money from them. That is a decision left for you to make.

"When they lend you money, however, they will also give you conditions of borrowing and repayment to which you must adhere or else they will show you their unfriendly side.

"If I remember correctly, according to your balance sheet that we created many months ago at the beginning of this journey to financial freedom you have some loans right?"

"Yes", replied the Ellmases.

"Well, you must pay what you owe", Craig instructed them. "To you, parting with the money may be like life itself; but to the lenders, this is just business - so if you *must* borrow for any reason, do it with caution.

"Let's assume you have paid off all cards (credit and store) and you have one-month's living expenses saved away for emergencies, the next milestone is to **pay off all consumer debts**. This includes student loans, car loans, furniture loans etc. Generally, these are debts which were used to fund consumption (or lifestyle) rather than investment.

"A bank's loan advertisement that I saw recently goes like this:

> *'Whether you are ready for a new car, the pleasure a new boat can bring, to take that dream vacation you've always wanted or to consolidate your existing debt into*

a single manageable monthly payment, we can help make your dreams and plans a reality'.

"Friendly appeal isn't it? I have never thought it will be anybody's dream to become a slave (financially) to a lender. The lender's job is to advertise, you fall for it on your own accord and then pay back through your nose. So now is the time to pay off all of them – no matter how many and never go back down the same path again."

Bankruptcy Issues

"Craig, I have been talking to my sister, Jennifer, in the US, about what we are doing to get out of debt" Sally informed them. "She said if she ever gets to the point that she can't pay her mortgage together with loans and credit cards, she will declare herself bankrupt and won't have to pay the loans herself. Not that we will ever consider bankruptcy but what is your view on this. She asked of you, by the way."

"She did?" Craig said with a smile on his face as if remembering something. "How is she?"

"She's fine. She will be coming back to the UK to revamp her dormant company in an effort to expand her business empire to this side of the Atlantic."

"She seems to be doing well for herself. It'd be nice to see her again" Craig said nonchalantly.

"You will. Very soon" Sally said with assurance.

"You may be interested to know, my friend, that she's neither married nor engaged yet. She said she never had time for dating due to business demands" Desmond said, trying to re-ignite Craig's interest.

"She's not?" Craig sounded surprised. Almost dejectedly he added "Well I've made enough women mistakes to last me a lifetime."

"You two used to be an *item*; that was before 'Grace' happened", Sally chipped in.

"*Happened* is the right word to use. Please don't remind me. I've moved on from that long time ago."

"If that is true, it may be time for you to move to the next stage – find a good wife. After all Grace has been married (and divorced) twice *after* you."

"That's what I'm trying to avoid", Craig added in almost in frustration. "Remember also that Grace apparently has never been a Christian so she can do whatever she wants with her life. Anyway, enough about me, let's get back to the work at hand.

"Sally, what Jenny told you is true; but that is not the whole truth. Bankruptcy by definition as a legal proceeding that prohibits the debt collectors to collect debt from an individual who has been declared bankrupt by the court. The legal system ensures that the court only declares the individual who meets certain criteria and even then the individual has to pay certain debt such as student loans.

"Bankruptcy is an option that is often considered when individuals can no longer pay their debts as they fall due. Though for the people involved, bankruptcy provides relative 'peace of mind' from creditors' harassments, there are many more reasons why this may not be the way to go because in bankruptcy[4]:

- You cannot obtain credit for over £500 without informing the lender that you are bankrupt.

- You cannot act as a company director without the court's permission

- You cannot take any part in the promotion, formation or management of a limited company (LTD or LLC) without the permission of the court.

- You cannot trade in any business under any other name unless you inform all persons concerned of the bankruptcy.

- You may not work as an insolvency practitioner (an authorised debt specialist)

- You may be a trustee of a charity.

- You may not become a member of parliament.

- You may not become a member of the local authority.

- Your credit is affected for many years after the annulment.

- You may be publicly examined in court.

"A person declared bankrupt may be discharged (freed from obligations under the bankruptcy order) after one year. However, it may legally be on your all credit records for up to ten years. After discharge, you start afresh and may even begin to acquire assets again. Easy isn't it? But what happens to the people whose money you couldn't and didn't pay back?" Craig asked the Ellmases.

4
https://assets.publishing.service.gov.uk/government/uploads/system/uploads/attachment_data/file/902080/schedule_of_bankruptcy_restrictions_BRO_BRU.pdf

"The law says you're free from those debts, doesn't it?" Desmond answered.

"The fact that the law says it is okay does not mean it is alright as far as God is concerned. A Christian's word should be his/her bond. If you borrow money and you signed that you will repay it, then you have no alternative but to do it even though it may be lawful not to. If you do not, then according to Psalms 37: 21, you are 'wicked'".

> **"The wicked borrows and does not re-pay..."**
> Psalm 37:21 (The Bible)

"That's harsh, man" Desmond exclaimed.

"I didn't say it; the Bible did", Craig explained.

"Oh I see" Sally said, ignoring the two men. "If you will have to repay what you owe anyway as the Bible teaches, why go through the stress of bankruptcy and the stigma that goes with it?"

"Now you understand where I'm coming from, Sally. This is just what I believe. Rather than advocate bankruptcy, I can advise that people reduce expenses; maximise income; devise a debt management plan as soon as possible or even take a consolidation loan (yes I know but only if it will help in the avoidance of bankruptcy). The lenders will work with you if you assure them that you will pay them back; that way they know they will be repaid instead of losing their money through the bankruptcy route."

IVA (Individual Voluntary Arrangements)

"What about IVA? At least it is still better than bankruptcy?" Desmond asked.

"Ah yes", Craig replied. "IVA or Individual Voluntary Arrangement is a form of insolvency, which has some features of debt management programmes in it, that is used as a last resort to avoid bankruptcy, when debts become unmanageable. In this, a new repayment schedule is worked out with the creditors, but it has the crucial difference of being a legal process that is binding on all involved.

"To take out an IVA an individual needs to work with a certified insolvency practitioner, who will draw up a detailed outline of your current financial circumstances ‐ income, outgoings, assets, and debts. The courts will then use this outline to decide on an appropriate and affordable repayment plan, which if accepted by the creditors (or more accurately, providing none of them provide a compelling reason to reject it), takes on legal force. This means that all debt recovery proceedings from your creditors must cease, and providing you stick to the terms agreed, nothing else will happen.

"At the end of the IVA period, usually 5 years, any remaining debt is written off and you will be officially 'debt free'. During the period of the IVA, however, your financial options are strictly limited: you're not allowed to borrow any more money from any source, even if you could find a company willing to lend to you.

"Furthermore, if you fall behind in your payments, you will probably find that bankruptcy proceedings will quickly follow, as your creditors begin the fight to use any remaining assets you have to clear as much of their lending as possible.

"Even though this is better than bankruptcy, an IVA will stick out like a sore thumb on your credit file, and even when the IVA term is over, you may find it extremely difficult to get credit of any kind.

"If it's like that, how come they glamorise it on TV?" Sally asked with a baffled look on her face.

"That's the power of the media for you", Craig replied in conclusion.

Debt Snowball

"Okay, enough of that on the 5th Milestone; let's move along. We will deal with the different loans as we did with the credit cards; we will snowball the loans:

1. Make a list of all your loans starting with the one with the smallest balance. As before, don't look at the interest rate at this time. The only time the interest rate should come into play is if you have two balances that are very close.

2. Focus on paying off the loan with the smallest balance first by applying all the cash (you've been using in the last milestone to build your emergency fund) to that loan.

3. Once the first loan is paid off, you use the money you were paying on that loan and begin applying that to the balance of the next highest loan balance. Pay the second loan off and keep doing the same thing with the third, fourth etc. or until all the loans are paid off.

"While you're doing all these, keep making the usual monthly payment, to the other loans that you are not currently focusing on. Some lenders may penalise you for paying off the loans early. Do not let this deter you from paying them off. You will sleep better without the loans hanging over your head.

"Be aware that you may not be able to just top up loan payments like you did the credit cards. Some lenders may want you to pay the loan off at once. To do this, just save the money away for a few months while making the usual monthly payment. As soon as you have enough to pay off the loan completely, do it.

"If one of the loans is a car loan, once it has been paid off, you may want to continue making the same payment but this time to yourself in a separate account. The reason being that when you need a replacement car, your part-exchange (trade-in) and the money you have saved will be enough for you to get a new car without borrowing."

Borrowing Against Your House

"Instead of paying of all these loans one by one, why don't we just remortgage the house and add all the loans" Desmond asked "Many people are doing it and we have some equity on the house anyway."

"I have been expecting that question and I'm almost sure you would have guessed what my take will be on this. There are general pros and cons in borrowing against your home and they all need to be taken into consideration before you proceed with any additional borrowing.

"On the one hand, the money you can borrow on your home may be of a lower interest rate than most other forms of loans and this can help you to reduce your monthly repayments by using the equity for clearing more expensive debt. With the ability to spread the term of repayment over a much longer period, you can generally make quite an impact on reducing your monthly outgoings. This is not necessary in your case.

"From your Spending Plan, determine how much you are paying on all your outstanding debt and then calculate what the payments would be if they were all consolidated under the one loan against your house. This will show whether that is the best decision to make to help you manage your finances more easily. Also in areas where house prices are rising, the equity in the home would have increased and that will allow you to borrow more against it.

"On the other hand, if you are already struggling to make your home mortgage payments then, by borrowing more you will be putting your house on the line and you risk losing it. You certainly don't want the banks to foreclose on your loan or repossess your property. So if that looks probable, then it would be unwise to increase your borrowings.

"If you calculate that you will not be able to make the mortgage payments then it is better to sell off some unused (unneeded) items that you have to reduce debt elsewhere rather than risk losing your home.

"It might also be necessary to consider downsizing your home and buying something of a lower value so you can reduce your mortgage accordingly until you get your feet back on the ground. You heard Michael and Agatha talking about that yesterday.

"Your home may be your most valuable asset (when you pay off the mortgage and you gain complete ownership); and for some people, it is their ONLY valuable asset. You should always do all you possibly can to retain control of it. The decision on your asset is ultimately yours.

142

Craig shifted slightly on his chair and then continued by saying "From experience, I have learnt to change my habits rather than take the shortcut of consolidation. I once had a loan of £3500 and two credit cards. I can't actually tell you how it happened but after consolidating my cards and loan several times, I ended up with a loan of almost £25,000 and two maxed-out cards. What did I learn? Consolidation does not change your old financial habits; it only feeds them. You cannot borrow your way out of debt; you need financial education as well".

"Well now that you put it that way, I guess we'll just continue the one-loan-at-a-time system" Desmond said in resignation.

"You are already on the right path and what's more, you have a testimony, believe it or not. Like David fighting Goliath in the Bible, you can now say *the same the God who helped me when I was tackling the credit cards one-at-a-time will help me again with these loans one-at-a-time'*. Am I right?"

"You're quite right and thanks for the explanation" Sally answered.

"I think we'd better 'hit the sack' now so you guys can have time to see a bit more of Birmingham tomorrow before you return to London.

"Just one more thing; once you've paid off your loans, make a conscious effort to stay debt-free. Use only cash or a debit card for everyday purchases, and save up your money for big purchases like appliances and electronics and even cars. Yes, even cars. It has been done before, I have done it several times; it is still being done, and you can do it too."

Milestone #6

Increase Emergency Fund to Three Months' Living Expenses

Chapter 10

Emergency Fund – Level 3

The Ellmases last celebrated the completion of a Milestone months ago. Even though one was due today since they have now paid off their consumer debt; but it would have to wait – for a good reason.

While Sally was getting ready for their trip to the airport, Desmond was busy logging on to the Internet. It was Saturday and the Ellmases' next session with Craig was due in a few minutes.

"Hi guys" Craig said as soon as he saw the first blurry figure on his monitor. "I think you need to refocus your webcam."

"Sorry mate, these girls have been here again", Desmond responded as he proceeded to adjust the webcam and then asked "How's that Craig?"

"Much better."

"Sally we're on!" Desmond called out to his wife. Then in a lower tone Desmond said "guess who's arriving today ..."

Sally's entry into the room at that moment stopped Desmond in mid-sentence; she waved at Craig via the webcam before taking her seat.

"What are you both dressed up for?", Craig said wanting to know who's arriving.

"Jennifer is coming from the US this afternoon. We are going to pick her up from the airport once we've finished this session. Remember I told you a few months ago that she's coming back to the UK?" Sally replied.

"Yes you did" Craig replied. "Have no fear; this is a short session anyway; so let's begin now."

Increase Emergency Fund to Three Months' Living Expenses

"I must say that you guys are doing really well as you have been able to get rid of all credit and store cards; even your loans are now paid off. The next Milestone is for you to increase the Emergency Fund to three Months' living expenses.

"I know, at this stage, you may be itching to start investing or start paying off your mortgage but I assure you that this milestone is vital. Just stick with it. There are a lot of things you can profitably do with your money now that you are not slaving to pay some lender somewhere.

"The milestone is almost as easy as the Milestone #4; the only difference is that it may take a little longer to reach.

"At this point on your journey to financial freedom, you need to use ALL the cash flow you've been using previously to clear your loans to bring the emergency fund up to three-month worth of living expenses. Won't it be good to know that whatever happens, you can survive for almost one-hundred days on the same living standard without panicking?"

"Yeah, that would be nice but at the same time we'll pray that nothing disastrous happens" Sally said, agreeing with Craig.

"I have heard of people who build up their emergency fund to six months or even a year's worth of living expenses, why are you recommending only three months?" Desmond asked.

"I know I have been talking about three months as far as emergency fund is concerned but this is the absolute minimum if you don't want to be one emergency away from going into debt again. When you get to that level, you have a bit of breathing space to move on to build your wealth with God's help and to His glory. Most financial experts will tell you to build up three-to-six-months' emergency fund; you can build it up further if you wish. Whatever you do, have at least three months' worth of living expenses saved away. You may add an Emergency fund category to your Spending Plan so as to increase it further. Words won't be able to describe how good it will feel to know you have funds to cover you when an emergency actually occurs! Does that answer your question?" Craig asked.

"Yeah, thank you", Desmond responded.

"Okay then", Craig started again. "Once you've got the fund built, review it about once a year and consider topping up the amount if life events - like a new baby, new house or new salary etc - have increased your spending in any way. Resist the temptation to use the fund for anything other than unexpected, necessary expenses. The rule here is to LOOK BUT DON'T TOUCH."

"That which we persist in doing becomes easier not that the nature of the task has changed, but our ability has increased."

- Ralph Waldo Emerson

Using Overdraft for Emergencies

After a short pause, Craig continued by saying "I always enjoy it when I get to this point with anyone I take through this Milestones of Financial Freedom. By now you have seen changes in your lives and you now have focus and all your energy is directed towards your goals. So I don't get many questions here."

"Not this time Bro" Desmond said, feeling pleased with himself.

"Craig, I understand what you're saying about emergency fund; but I have been wondering; can't we just use our overdraft facilities whenever an emergency strikes instead of keeping lots of money in the bank?" Desmond asked.

"You can but I won't advice you to. The reasons being, these emergencies will be yours - not the banks. Due to the impermanent and informal nature of overdrafts, they're not regulated in the same way as credit cards or personal loans; so the banks may decide to withdraw the overdraft facility just before you need it. The vast majority of banks state in their terms and conditions that an overdraft facility can be revoked at any time. So if you have an emergency at that particular time, you are forced to arrange for it afresh (doubling your trouble). Time is usually of the essence when it comes to emergencies.

"Another reason I discourage this route is that while it may seem to provide you, the consumers, with a semi-permanent income 'extension', an overdraft is an expensive, insecure and unpredictable way to borrow. If you spend beyond overdraft limit you'll be hit with bank charges, believe me. I once went over my limit by £1.25 and the bank charged me £25! Ouch! £23.75 worth of ouch!!

"If you allow your bank balance to stay negative past the overdraft cancellation date, it's likely you'll be hit with bank charges also -- and all these will push you further into 'the red'.

"If, like many others, you've become accustomed to ignoring the little minus sign in front of your bank balance, now is the time for a re-think; the minus sign means 'not yours'. This, in any case, is another financial habit that you need to break – so do it now for the sake of your freedom!!

"Getting over using your overdraft might be tough, but it can be done.... I have done it. I used to swim in the red ink of my overdraft facilities; I had to deliberately cut down (by about £50) on how far into it I go each month until I finally got out and stopped using it completely. And strangely, without this supposed 'safety net', my finances became far more secure because my emergency fund became mine instead of the banks' and I get paid interest in addition."

"Does that answer your question Desmond?"

"Oh yes. It seems as if you were waiting for me to ask that question" Desmond answered, a bit surprised at the depth of knowledge he just received.

"Not really, that's' just the way it is" Craig told him.

"Guys, I think we need to be heading toward the airport now, you never know what the traffic might be like." Sally said breaking the banter that seemed to be developing.

"I may be seeing you people very soon. There are some business opportunities *cooking* down there in London for me. Have a nice trip." Craig said smiling as he logged off.

151

Chapter 11

Money in Its Three Phases

In the months since he started coaching his friends, Desmond and Sally, Craig Lamu had been working on acquiring some businesses in London. So while he was in town, the Ellmases invited him to Saturday lunch.

After Craig and Desmond had taken their seats at the dining table, Sally proceeded to show the good works she had been doing in the kitchen all day. Craig's eyes nearly popped out of their sockets when Sally came back to the dining area. No, the reaction was not at the sight of the food; but because of the lady coming behind Sally from the kitchen - Jennifer Goldsmith.

Jennifer was a beautiful and smart business woman formerly based in Cleveland, Ohio in the US. Being Sally's junior sister, she had known Craig through his many visits to the Goldsmiths' residence with Desmond. If fact they went out a few times together in their college days. Craig thought himself blessed and highly-favoured that he planned to spend this weekend in London after he finished from his 3-day conference at Eastbourne on the South Eastern coast of England.

The day began with Desmond picking Craig up from his hotel in the morning. They both went to play a round of golf at Desmond's club where he had re-registered after two years of being on 'money-diet' while he put his finances back under control. On their way back to Craig's hotel they passed by the Emirate Stadium which Craig has not visited since it was opened many years ago. Craig could not just miss the opportunity of visiting Arsenal Football Club's 'holy ground' on this visit to London.

Later after freshening up at the hotel, Craig went with Desmond for the lunch which Sally was preparing at home and for the 'surprise' which she also promised him.

Desmond prayed over the meal and the four spent the mealtime making small talk. Jennifer and Craig tried to catch up with each other's businesses after so many years of not seeing each other.

After the meal, Sally thanked Craig again (for the umpteenth time) for helping them out of their now paid-off credit card debt and several loans. "I still can't believe that all it took was just common-sense and determination to get out from under the clutches of debt".

"You must have a source of income as well and you guys have two; which is very good in the world we live in now. One of the reasons why many people get into financial difficulties is that they don't understand money or how it works – apart from the fact that they are working for it and using it to buy 'stuff'.

"Simply put, there are three phases of money; no matter which currency you happen to be using. The phase you are operating in, will determine the name of the money you are spending. Basically we have:

- Survival Money
- Smart Money
- Sweet Money

"Sweet money; I like the sound of that" Desmond said, looking up as if in dreamland.

"Don't jump the gun. Let me explain each of them and how they relate to our milestones."

"I too will have to wait until you've finished then because I have some questions myself" Jennifer spoke for the first time since Craig started talking to them as a group.

"No problem. Once you feel the question burning within you, just let it out" Craig said to her without looking directly at her.

Survival Money

"This is the phase of money we have been dealing with up to this point. This is the money you need for all your monthly expenses including food, shelter, clothing, insurances etc. as well as your emergency fund. You cannot even think of building wealth without having your survival money in place.

"Everybody has survival money - no matter how little you make. Unfortunately some people only ever have survival money because of little income or maybe they just don't completely escape the 'debt cycle'. The usual problem is that many people use their survival money as if it were sweet or 'play' money. They buy luxury items by adding to money they already owed to financial institutions; binding themselves further to the slavery of debt. By so doing, they won't have the fund needed to transcend their survival money into smart money.

"To move your finances to the next level, you will need to have a different outlook on life where you understand the difference between needs, wants and desires.

"Needs are those factors that are required to maintain good health in mind and body for you and those whom you are responsible for. Needs are your necessary purchases such as food, shelter (rent or mortgage), clothing etc.

"Wants involve choices when you want to buy brand-name items instead of generic ones. Putting alloy wheels on your car instead of normal wheels is a want just as getting the latest design clothes as opposed to normal clothes is a want.

"Desires are items that can be purchased AFTER all other obligations have been met and if there are surplus funds available. If not kept in check, these are the things that get people into trouble. These are the things that cause your debt and stress. These are the things that make people miserable at the end of the day because you still have to pay for them, you don't need them and you certainly don't need the debt that comes with them.

"Also as you may have experienced the lows of constant financial stress due to the pressure of debt, you will not want to go back there in a hurry. Overall you will need to develop a mind-set to stay out of debt.

"You should have also adopted an attitude whereby you will only ever spend less money than you earn and where you will never buy luxury or non-essential items if you have to go into debt to get them. This should continue so you can move to the next level where you have additional money that can be used for investment."

Smart Money

Craig took a deep breath and smiled before continuing. "It is a great feeling to get on top of your debt and know that you are able to make all your payments each month and not have to worry about debt collectors or paying for your groceries. However, now is not the time to stop doing the things that have helped turn your lives around.

"Continuing along the proven path to financial security of reducing debt and managing the daily flow of your cash will give you a lot more freedom to build wealth now rather than focusing all your energy on reducing debt. It is a more positive phase in your life and you will see how much the debt encroached on your lifestyle and freedom.

"I have told you previously that personal finance is more personal than it is financial. Nowhere is it more evident than in the smart use of money. Smart money is the fund that you have available for investment and for adding financial security to your life as you age. What you do from now on depends on your goals, age and family situation, how much you have to invest and how long you want to invest for. We will deal with this in a later session.

"You will only consider borrowing if it is to buy an appreciating asset that will deliver you more return for your money than the amount you are paying in interest. This may be in the form of getting a rental property as part of your investment portfolio; where the rent you receive is more than the monthly running costs of the property including the mortgage, service charge(s) and insurance This new attitude will also include better time management skills and that in turn will give you more time to do the things that you like.

Sweet Money

"This is the best of the lot. Not many people get to earn or use money in this phase and those who do, they get it from their investments. It is generally called 'Passive, Residual or Portfolio income'. This is money that an individual derives on a regular basis, with little effort required to maintain; he or she is not actively involved. It may be in the form of:

- Profit on rent collected from properties;

- Royalties from publishing a book or from a patented material or invention;

- Earnings from internet advertisement on your websites;

- Earnings from a business that does not require direct involvement from the owner or merchant;

- Dividend and interest income from owning securities, such as stocks and bonds. This is Portfolio Income.

"Sweet money is the money that you've made from your money – if you've used it smartly through investment. In the early years, smart investors use this money again as smart money; they re-invest it. But in the later years in life, it is generally used as income.

"Aim for sweet money and use it to improve your lives and of those around you. Your generosity at this stage will no longer be subject to any employer's pay packet and you can serve God whole-heartedly.

> "Money is like manure; it's not worth a thing unless it's spread around encouraging young things to grow."
>
> - Thornton Wilder

"Your forthcoming wealth can be used for the comfort and enrichment of your family, to meet the needs of others, and to spread the Gospel throughout the world. On the other hand, it can be used for destructive purposes – many of which we have seen all over the world.

"Your attitude determines how your wealth is used. Let your attitudes be those that will be acceptable to God in the light of

His Word. Remember that if you use what's in your hands to do what God wants, your hands will always be full. Keep up those good attitudes and financial habits as God increases your wealth to His glory."

"May I ask my question now, Pastor Craig?" Jennifer asked as Craig paused a bit. She has been pleasantly surprised at the 'new Craig' sitting across the table from her.

"Yes, by all means" Craig answered.

"Why is it so necessary to be free of credit cards and loans before you start investing fully?" Jennifer asked, not really in tune with this new way of becoming financially-free. "I have credit card balances but I'm also investing. What is wrong with that?"

"Good question Jenny and there is nothing wrong with your style. My belief has always been **'Get yourself into good financial shape – and then enhance your financial situation with sound investments'**. It doesn't make sense, to me anyway, to start investing if your bank balance is always running low or if you are struggling to pay your necessary monthly expenses. Your investment funds will be better spent to rectify adverse financial issues that affect you each day.

"Every investment carries an element of risk and you cannot, while your money is still in survival phase, afford to lose money an unfortunate turn in investment. Instead you need to use the funds to eliminate debt once and for all - survival comes first.

"Even though those times of debt-elimination may be extremely difficult for most people, the process of reversing your monetary situation is an education that will set you up for better things in the future. So while you are in the process of clearing up your present financial situation, make it a point of duty to educate yourself about the various types of

159

investments; which was what I did. That way, when you are in a good shape financially, you will be armed with the knowledge that you need to make sound investment decisions concerning your future."

"Does that answer your question Jenny?" Sally asked as everyone waited anxiously for Jennifer's reaction to Craig's explanation.

"Yes – for now" Jennifer replied. "I'm sure I will have more questions after I've gone through your notes again". Jennifer has apparently been reading the notes her sister has made over the last 2 years during their 'Milestone sessions' with Craig.

"No problem Jenny, take your time. I just hope I'll be able to answer you rightly" Craig added.

"Craig. What was the outcome of the business meeting you had in the City on Wednesday?" Desmond asked, changing the subject abruptly.

"Oh it was profitable; the price is right. I think I will start the 'due diligence' process next week" Craig offered in reply.

"What are you boys talking about?" Sally asked curiously at the sudden change in subject.

"Oh Craig is looking to buy a Sports shop in the City to add to his chain" Desmond offered.

"So you are a big business man now, *ehn* Craig?" Jennifer asked smile at discovering this new side of Craig.

"Well, I've been known to dabble in a few things" Craig responded clearly enjoying the interest Jennifer is showing in his work. "I guess you guys will be seeing more of me in London in the next few months while I complete some transactions."

160

Milestone #7

Pay Off Your Mortgage

&

Save For Major Expenses

Chapter 12

Pay Off Home Mortgage and Save For Major Purchases

Craig's company had been given the opportunity to purchase two more sports' shop businesses in London since he closed on his latest acquisition two weeks earlier. It had become inevitable that he would be spending a lot more time in London than in Birmingham or Sydney for the next six months, so he decided to move into one of his rental properties in West London that just became vacant.

The Ellmases went to see the new flat as well as have their next session with Craig. Since it was Saturday, Jennifer came along out of curiosity of the content of this session and also to 'check out Craig's pad' – her words exactly.

"Welcome to the second phase of your journey to financial freedom. This second part of the journey is much more enjoyable than the first; in that the pressure brought about by debt is no longer an issue except for the mortgage of course. You can now concentrate on building wealth your way but for God's glory. Your generosity can now also rise to a higher level as God begins to prosper you more."

This was how Craig opened the 'Smart Phase' of the journey to financial freedom as he puts it.

The 10-10-10-70 Plan

"Desmond, Sally; I'm going to add a twist to your Spending Plan from this point on. Without credit card or loan payments, your disposable income or cash flow should be substantial every month - all things being equal. You need to start using it again only this time instead of eliminating debt you will be building wealth.

"Let me introduce you to the 10-10-10-70 Plan. It is really simple; your income should be divided up into the following:

- 10% - Tithe (or charitable giving)
- 10% - Investment for Retirement
- 10% - Saving for Major Purchases
- 70% - To live on

"I use this plan to keep my clients on their toes. The reason being that the absence of those 'killer' credit card and loan payments can entice people to 'beef-up' their expenses thus leading to the reduction of their cash flow. You should continue in the habit of living below your means if you really want to build wealth.

"The first 10% is the Tithe. We have already dealt with that issue earlier so there is no need going over it again.

"The second 10% which is for investing for retirement should go toward building an investment portfolio which will grow as you two get older. You may start small first (or test the waters as they say) before you commit fully into any aspect of investment you choose. That way you may minimise your losses (if it occurs) and you won't develop high blood pressure due to anxiety. How you invest will depend on your age, goals, family situation, disposable income etc. We will deal with this fully in the next session.

"The third 10% can be used for several things depending on your wishes. You should include paying off your home mortgage as one of them. Others can be saving for major expenses such as your children's university education, starting a new business etc. Do you remember the goals we set at the beginning of this Journey to Financial Freedom?"

"Yes, yes" Desmond replied a fraction of second faster than Sally, urging Craig to continue.

"Some of them can be accomplished quickly here; just keep in mind your needs, wants and desires.

"The final 70% should cover your normal monthly expenses as usual."

"What if it doesn't?" Desmond asked this time.

"Make adjustments. You should be used to that by now. You made adjustments to become free of your credit cards and loans; you can make similar adjustments to become totally financially free.

Pay Off Home Mortgage

"You would have called me crazy if, one year ago, I had asked you to try to pay off your home mortgage. But now that you have no credit card debt or consumer loans, you can. There is life after debt; many people just don't experience it.

"To become totally debt-free, you will need to pay off your home mortgage amongst other things."

"Hold it, hold it" Jennifer said holding up her hands. "Don't you know you'll be missing investing opportunities if you use the money to pay off your mortgage? In the United States the interest on your mortgage is tax deductible. This tax deduction may mean considerable savings for many homeowners especially those in the higher tax bracket. If you pay off your mortgage, you'll lose the interest deduction. What do you say to that?"

With three pairs of eyes staring intensely at him Craig smiled and said "I don't know which one you value more; your total financial freedom or saving a few thousand pounds annually from your taxes. You must ask yourself if you are thinking in the long-term or just short-term. The way you feel about debt will affect your decision on this matter. The question now is: what will pay you more in the long run? Here are my reasons for advocating for paying off my mortgage early:

1. Paying off your mortgage provides emotional relief from the anxiety of owing money. The simple feeling of owning your home free and clear is reason enough. This sense of security may matter even more if you plan to live in your home when you retire. You get cash in your pocket if you decide to downgrade in your later years. Also, you may desire to leave a debt-free home to your heirs – watch out for the tax implications of that.

2. Without a mortgage payment, you'll have more money to invest for the future. Your retirement savings can grow more quickly. Mortgage interest on a large or high-rate loan may be costing you a hefty sum. Instead of paying interest, you could be earning interest with your funds.

3. Paying off your mortgage removes loan-related stresses, too; you will sleep well at night. Houses gain and lose value, depending on local conditions. These market changes affect the equity you've built

166

in your home. Without a loan, you remove the risk of negative equity (owing more on your property than its current value). Also, you avoid being affected by rising rates if the interest on your mortgage is variable.

4. Stewardship Issues. We are stewards of God's resources. Throwing money down the drain in interest payments on our mortgages and doing nothing about it is not good stewardship in my opinion. Aim to pay off the mortgage long BEFORE the allotted term.

5. Apart from all the above. I have never met anyone who ever regretted paying off their mortgage early.

"It's about time we moved away from the herd-mentality that says we must carry a mortgage to full-term; let's do what will please God with our money. **There is life after debt.**"

"Okay, okay. I get the general idea. You may continue" Jennifer said dismissing the explanation with a wave of the hand.

"So how do we best go about paying off the mortgage" Sally asked quickly feeling slightly embarrassed by her sister's attitude.

"The most common way is to attack it head-on by topping-up your monthly payments. Take for example, a £140,000, 25-year mortgage at 5.5%. If your monthly payment is £860, you will pay just under £118,000 in interest during the term of the mortgage.

"If you add only £100 to the monthly payment, you will shave 4 years and 10 months off from the mortgage term and pay only about £92,000 in interest.

"Add an extra £50 to that and the term saved becomes 6 years and 7 months and you only pay £83,000 in interest.

"There are several other strategies that you can use to rapidly pay off your mortgage depending on the complexity of your mortgage and its conditions. With your current cash flow, you can actually consistently make overpayments monthly thereby chiselling away at both the term and the interest paid on your mortgage while you still carry on with your investment for retirement without any problem."

"I like the sound of that" Desmond said, sounding satisfied.

"Just get out your calculators and determine what amount goes where; adjust your Spending Plan to be able to live on 70% of your income and you are well on your way.

Save For Major Expenses

"Let me just touch quickly on the saving for major expenses. Once you know that you're on track with investing for retirement and that your home is being rapidly paid-off, you can start to think about your other goals. One word of caution please; do not use your emergency fund for any of these. I have discovered that people tend to do this.

"The major expenses maybe: your children' university tuition, the new kitchen you've always wanted, your big 25th wedding anniversary, another baby ..."

"No way *José*" Sally interrupted standing with her palms facing Craig as if she was blocking whatever is coming from him. "We've finished in that department. It's over to you now."

"Well we shall see. Anyway, what you do here and with these savings will depend on your original goals. Just don't do too many things at the same time or you may become overwhelmed and not accomplish much.

"One thing I know is that without any debt hanging around your neck, you can do a lot more than you've ever thought. **There really is life after debt.**

"That is all for now; any questions?", Craig asked looking around. When everybody shook their heads, he continued "My Saturday in two weeks' time is free; I can come over to your place if it's alright with you all and we'll have the next session on investments and other stuff then. What do you say?"

"It's alright by me" Desmond replied before turning to his wife and sister-in-law to say "Ladies?"

Milestone #8

Invest for Retirement

Chapter 13

Investing 101

Craig has been informed that Mrs Helena Goldsmith, Sally and Jennifer' mother, was 'in town' and would be visiting the Ellmases on the same day he had to have a session with them. Helena, a widow of many years, was visiting especially because she had not seen Jennifer since she returned from the US to build the UK side of her business.

The last time Craig met Mrs Goldsmith, was during Sally and Desmond's wedding many years ago. Craig was convinced, for reasons known only to him, that Helena had a certain dislike for him. He just wasn't sure he was up to meeting her that afternoon at all; so he devised a plan. He decided to go and see the Ellmases early; and leave before the time Mrs Goldsmith was due to arrive.

Sally on the other hand, had hinted her mum of the relationship blossoming once again between Craig and Jennifer. This prompted the older woman to arrive a little earlier than planned so she could have enough time to hear all about Jennifer's travels, her businesses and meet this *new* Craig.

Craig's early arrival didn't take the Ellmases by surprise as he had called Desmond on Friday about his plan. So after all the greetings, Craig started the session for the day as quickly as he could.

Why You Should Invest

Without wasting too much time on pleasantries, Craig launched into the lesson of the day. He began by saying "Investing has become increasingly important over the years, as the future of social security benefits, in the western world where they are operated, becomes unknown.

"People want to insure their future but they know that if they are depending on Social Security benefits, they may be in for a rude awakening. By that time, they may no longer have the ability to earn a steady income. Investing is the answer to the financial unknowns of the future with God's guidance.

"You have been saving money in a low interest savings account over the years. Now, you want to see that money grow at a faster rate. Investing is also a way of attaining the things that you want, such as a college education for your children, or some expensive 'toys'. Of course, your financial goals will determine what type of investing you do. The power of compound interest worked AGAINST you in months past, you can now have the opportunity to make it work FOR you.

"Not that this is your case, but if you want or need to make a lot of money fast, you would be more interested in higher risk investing, which will give you a larger return (or loss) in a shorter amount of time. If you are saving for something in the far off future, such as retirement, you would want to make safer investments that grow over a longer period of time.

"The overall purpose in investing is to create wealth and security, over a period of time. It is important to remember that you will not always be able to earn a wage... you will eventually want to retire.

"As we have seen with the many companies that have suffered financial collapse, you also cannot necessarily depend on your

174

company's retirement plan either. So, again, investing is the key to insuring your own financial future, but you must make smart investments!"

What Are Your Investment Goals?

"When it comes to investing, many first time investors want to jump right in with both feet. Unfortunately, very few of those investors are successful. Investing in anything requires some degree of skill and knowledge. It is important to remember that few investments are a sure thing – there is the risk of losing your money! The best way to defeat the fear of failure is to gain some knowledge.

"Before you jump right in, it is better to not only find out more about investing and how it all works, but also to re-evaluate what your goals are. What do you hope to achieve with your investments? Will you be funding a college education? Buying a home? Retiring? Before you invest a single penny, really think about what you hope to achieve with that investment. Knowing what your goal is will help you make smarter investment decisions along the way! A wise old man that I know said *'Invest your time before you invest your money to get the best return'.*

"Too often, people invest money with dreams of becoming rich overnight. This is possible – but it is also rare. It is usually a very bad idea to start investing with hopes of becoming rich overnight. It is safer to invest your money in such a way that it will grow slowly over time. However, if your investment goal is to get rich quick, you should learn as much about high-yield, short term investing as you possibly can before you invest.

"Are you saying get-rich-quick investments are permissible under this milestone?" Desmond asked.

"Not exactly. Some people may want that option but I won't recommend it for you. I always equate get-rich-quick investing with gambling as it leaves no room for proper research and you have more chance of losing than winning.

"You should strongly consider talking to a financial planner before making any investments. Your financial planner can help you determine what type of investing you must do to reach the financial goals that you have set. He or she can give you realistic information as to what kind of returns you can expect and how long it will take to reach your specific goals.

"Again, remember that investing requires more than calling a broker and telling them that you want to buy stocks or bonds. It takes a certain amount of research and knowledge about the market if you hope to invest successfully."

"Hello Craig", said a voice from the bedroom area. Mrs Helena Goldsmith stood in the doorway leading to the guest section of the house. Obviously, she had been in the house for some time and had listened to what Craig had been saying before revealing her presence. Recognising the voice, Craig stood up immediately to greet Helena. With his friends trying not to even hide their amusement at what was going on, he knew he had been set-up. Helena was a beautiful woman of African descent and she enjoyed showing that off in the way she dressed. She was a brilliant businesswoman in her late fifties, who single-handedly raised her two daughters from their teenage years when she lost her husband.

"Good afternoon Mrs Goldsmith" Craig said greeting her "it is nice to see you again."

"Good afternoon to you too" Helena responded.

"I didn't know you've ... eh ... arrived ..." Craig apologised sheepishly and then turned to his friends while saying behind

176

clenched teeth "… some people decided to suppress that information!"

"It's alright, I understand. I must confess, I like what I've heard you say since you came in here" Helena commented, sensing what was going on among the friends but trying very hard to keep from laughing.

"Carry on; don't let me stop you but I hope you don't mind if I just listen from here" Helena said moving towards where Jennifer was sitting just off Craig's line of sight.

"No, not at all Madam" Craig replied, feeling like a goldfish in a glass bowl.

Investment Strategies

Without making it too obvious, Craig took in a long deep breath and slowly let the air through his mouth before he continued. "Okay let's talk a bit about investment strategies. For the fact that investing is not a sure thing in most cases, it is much like a game – you don't know the outcome (even though you hope for a favourable one) until the game has been played. Whenever you play almost any type of game, you must have a strategy. Investing isn't any different – you need an investment strategy.

"An investment strategy is basically a plan for investing your money in various types of investments that will help you meet your financial goals in a specific amount of time. Each type of investment contains within itself other individual investments that you can choose from. For example, a clothing store sells clothes – but those clothes consist of shirts, T-shirts, trousers, dresses, skirts, undergarments, etc. The stock market is a type of investment, but it contains different types of stocks, which all contain different companies that you can invest in.

"I told you earlier about doing your own research; if you haven't done yours, the stock market can quickly become very confusing – simply because there are so many different types of investments and individual investments to choose from. This is where your strategy, combined with your risk tolerance and investment style all come into play. We will talk about risk tolerance in a short while."

Craig looked around and asked "Any questions so far?"

Accepting the shaking of heads that he received as 'No', he continued. "Okay", Craig said, continuing. "Never invest money without having a goal and a strategy for reaching that goal! This is essential. Nobody hands his or her money over to anyone without knowing what that money is being used for and when they will get it back – if ever! If you don't have a goal, a plan, or a strategy, that is essentially what you are doing! Always start with a goal and a strategy for reaching that goal!

"Do you now understand why I asked you to set goals right at the beginning of this Journey to Financial Freedom?"

"What is your strategy Craig?" Helena asked abruptly catching Craig off-guard. Before he could say anything she added "You were married once, so what are your goals along that line?"

"Muuuum!!" Sally and Jennifer said in unison and in disbelief

"What? It's just an innocent question. Shush! Let him answer" Mrs Goldsmith said shutting her daughters up. Then turning back to Craig she said "Go on my dear" motioning to him.

Desmond just sat there quietly enjoying the whole 'show'. His mother-in-law seemed to be doing exactly what he had in mind for Craig that day. Up till this time he has been trying to summon the courage to talk to his rich-bachelor friend about his plans of having a wife; especially with Jennifer in the picture.

"It was never in my plans to become divorced at all..." Craig began in response, "... but Grace, my ex-wife, loved my money more than she loved me. We both encouraged each other to (foolishly) buy whatever we liked, whenever we liked them until we could no longer even borrow money again. We were up to our eyeballs in debt and our house was full of things we didn't need which we bought with the money we didn't have; just to impress the people we didn't like.

"After the death of my father and while I was settling his estate, Grace hit me, out of the blues, with divorce papers. That was after she had cleaned out both our house and our joint-account. I was left penniless. I didn't contest anything because the only thing we had were debts of all sorts. Apart from that, it was finally revealed that she was never a Christian like I thought she was. I went to Australia to have some time away from everybody and everything. When I returned to the UK two years later, I moved to Birmingham to start afresh.

"To answer your question Madam, one of my goals was to pay off all my debt and NEVER go back into debt again. My strategy worked so well that I became debt-free in four years and now I'm financially-free also. Now that that has been accomplished, I intend to get married but this time to a woman who would love me as well as love the Lord."

"That was a good answer. Lots of details, but good" Helena said after Craig stopped talking. "What do you mean by being 'financially-free'?"

"It means I have enough passive income coming in every month to take care of all my monthly expenses.", Craig answered quickly. "It means I don't really have to work if I choose; my investments are now feeding me – so to speak. Mind you, I will not stop working as I don't want to become a lazy busybody as described in the bible (2 Thessalonians 3:11). As long as I have the strength to produce funds for the Kingdom of God, I will keep doing it."

> **"For we hear that there are some which walk among you disorderly, working not at all, but are busybodies..."**
> 2 Thessalonians 3:11 (The Bible)

Determine Your Risk Tolerance

Taking Helena's silence as a sign to continue, Craig went on. "Let's get to investments, shall we?". "For investment, each individual has a risk tolerance that should not be ignored. Any good stockbroker or financial planner knows this, and they should make the effort to help you determine what your risk tolerance is. Then, they should work with you to find investments that do not exceed your risk tolerance.

"Determining one's risk tolerance involves several different things: age, how much money you have to invest, income requirements etc. Risk tolerance is the degree of uncertainty that an investor can handle in regard to a negative change in the value of his or her portfolio.

"For instance, if you've invested in the stock market and you watch the movement of that stock daily. If your stock begins dropping slightly, what would you do? Would you sell out or would you let your money ride? If you have a low tolerance for risk, you would want to sell out... if you have a high tolerance, you would let your money ride and see what happens. This is not based on what your financial goals are. This tolerance is based on how you feel about your money!

"A 70-year-old retiree will generally have a lower risk tolerance than a single 30-year-old executive, who generally has a longer time frame to make up for any losses incurred on his or her portfolio."

"May I say something please" Mrs Goldsmith said, moving her chair forward.

"Oh no, not again Mum!" Jennifer exclaimed, giving her mother the please-don't-embarrass-me look.

"Yes, you may Madam" replied Craig, feeling a little tingling of sweat developing under his shirt.

"Yes, we are 'all ears'" added Desmond as he stretched his legs out in front of him with his hand clamped together at the back of his head; mischievously grinning from ear to ear as if waiting for the *Clash of the Titans* to commence.

Turning to her daughters, Mrs Goldsmith said "How did you girls think you were able to spend four years each in the university without so many struggles?"

"We had enough in Dad's Life Insurance policy pay out" Sally replied tentatively.

"And...?" Mrs Goldsmith quipped.

"Don't look at me I don't know" Jennifer said to her sister.

"Actually that was it", Helena Goldsmith said bluntly. "I didn't have any business at that time. I was working as a company secretary back then. After your father passed away, we had no savings but thank God we received the Life Insurance payment. There were all sorts of suggestions from well-meaning people on what I should do with the money. I heard them ALL but I did not act on ANY until I knew what I was doing. I guess you could say my risk tolerance at that time was extremely low.

"My goal was to make the money last long enough for the two of you to complete your university education. I knew keeping the money in the bank wouldn't make it grow as quickly as I wished, so I started reading up on everything I could about money management and investments. At that time I was on leave-of-absence from my job; to be able to both grieve and tidy up my husband's business affairs – with the help of your uncle George of course.

"Since I had the time and to keep myself busy, I started decorating halls and baking cakes for people's birthday, other celebrations in church and so on. After sampling my cakes, Bose, George's wife, advised me to also start baking smaller cakes which could easily fit into lunch-boxes. I did and she helped me start my customer base. George on the other hand, advised me to start a company under which I would be carrying out my business in readiness for imminent expansion. Needless to say, I never returned to my old job and the rest is history. I ended up buying into some of the companies that were supplying me materials in the early days. Well, that's a story for another day.

"On the investment front, before I could invest for you girls, I first made sure we had enough to live on. Then I put some aside for anything unexpected that might crop up – people refer to it as 'Emergency Fund' these days. Am I right?"

"Yes, you are right" Craig said quickly, allowing himself a little smile.

It was now Desmond's turn to look, open-mouthed, as if he was watching an illusionist in action. He could not believe what he was hearing. Helena and Craig were actually *singing from the same hymn-sheet?*

"Thank you Craig", Helena said as she continued. "What I did next was to buy some bonds – first government bond (Gilts) and later some Corporate bonds. My initial venture into the stock market was to buy mutual funds for a long time before I started buying stock in individual companies.

"Using my new found knowledge and with God's help, I was able to even turn the one rental property your father and I had into four! So you see it was just the Life insurance to start with but it multiplied with investment. According to Craig, I can say I am financially-free now."

"Mum, why haven't you told us of this before...?" Sally asked. "...or at least teach us how to invest early?"

"I had you girls in mind all the time, I couldn't bother you with such things; you had to study. Besides that you were still under-age when I started. I guess I should have been doing all these things WITH you instead of just FOR you so we could all learn together."

"You ladies should be happy at least you had the Life Insurance payment to start with. My mother and I did not have such luxury", Craig said with his head bowed slightly. "When my father died, there was no Life Insurance payment but lots of debt to contend with. After taking care of all his debt without having to sell the house, a guy of whom I have never heard before then surfaced; claiming to be my brother (from another woman of course) and wanting HIS share of the *inheritance* - namely the house. It was during the court battle to save the house for my mother that Grace served me with divorce papers.

It was just too much. I had to get away and I lost contact with lots of people including you guys."

"Thank God for Class Reunions" Desmond said before his attention was called.

"Desmond, do you remember one Saturday morning that I called you from Australia and we talked about Life Insurance and Wills?"

"How can I forget?", Desmond responded. "I remember you woke up me from my beauty sleep at 6am!!"

"Forgive me for that my friend but I hope you now know my reason for that. I emphasis having Life Insurance and a Will to anyone I take through the Journey to Financial Freedom."

> "Don't let someone else create your world for you, for when they do they will always make it too small."
>
> - Edwin Louis Cole

Investment Alternatives

Turning to Mrs Goldsmith, Craig said "From what you told us earlier, ma'am, we can deduce that we have several levels of investments and that those that we choose will depend on our risk tolerance."

"That's quite right" Mrs Goldsmith said nodding her head.

"The different levels of investments we know now include stocks, bonds, properties, businesses, and cash. Sounds simple, right?" Craig asked.

"Right" the others replied in unison, waiting to see what he was getting at.

"Well, unfortunately, it gets more complicated as we go up in levels. You see, each type of investment has numerous types of investments that fall under it. Generally, we have:

Savings Accounts

"Savings accounts, which are the lowest forms of investment, can earn you interest with no risk. Since banks are already covered by the Financial Services Compensation Scheme[5] which protects 100% of the first £85,000 in any bank account for each customer (so joint accounts will be guaranteed up to £170,000) if a bank does go bust in the UK. In the US, the FDIC insures deposits (single & joint) up to $250,000. Deposits in Irish banks are 100% protected by a government guarantee. Money market savings accounts earn even better rates of interest.

"The **ISA** (Individual Saving Account), in the UK, is an account that shelters the interest from government taxation. Every taxpayer should open one – never leave any income on the table

"A **CD** (certificate of Deposit, also called a Time Deposit) offers higher interest, but you must leave the deposit in the account for a specified period of time."

---

[5] https://www.fscs.org.uk/what-we-cover/

Bonds

"Bonds are similar to Certificates of Deposit. Instead of being issued by banks, bonds are issued by the Government. When you buy a bond from a corporation, municipality, or government agency, the issuer promises to repay the value of the bond, plus interest, at a specific time. Firms such as Standard & Poor's and Moody's Investor Services rate bonds based on the credit worthiness of the issuer. The lower the risk, the lower interest rate you can expect to earn."

Mutual Funds

"Mutual funds are also relatively safe although they are a bit riskier than bonds. Mutual funds exist when a group of investors pool their money together to buy stocks, bonds, or other investments.

"A mutual fund owns shares in a number of companies to minimise risk. An indexed fund owns stock in all the companies listed in a particular index, such as the FTSE 100, Dow Jones Industrial Average or Standard & Poor's 500 Index. In an actively managed fund, the managers pick the stocks the fund will invest in; hence, individual investors are relieved of the responsibility of having to decide what stocks to buy."

Stocks

"Stocks are a vehicle I usually recommend for long term investments. Shares of stock are essentially shares of ownership in the company you are investing in. Owning shares of stock in a corporation makes you a part-owner of that company; even if it is a very tiny part. When the company does well financially, the value of your stock rises. However, if a company is doing poorly, your stock value drops. Stocks, of course, are even riskier than Mutual funds.

"Stockholders can make money in two ways. The firm may pay a dividend to stockholders. If the stock increases in value, it could be sold at a profit. There is no guarantee of either."

Starting Your Own Business

"Owning a small business can be a worthwhile investment provided you are willing to put the time and energy into the venture. It is risky as most small businesses fail within five years; so it is not everybody's *cup of tea.*

"Your business may be one you start from scratch or if you have the knowledge or can get the assistance, you may buy already established businesses. Whichever one you choose, just make sure it does not consume all of your time or you will become a slave to your business."

Real Estate

"Real estate has risen dramatically in value in many areas of the world in recent years, generally making home ownership a good investment. Owning rental properties can also be profitable. However, owning and managing rental properties can be a lot of work; that i can tell you from experience. It can also be costly, since properties must be maintained and there may also be period when there won't be any income at all. No tenant, no rent, no income. If you are considering rental properties as an investment, you need to do your homework well before you make your decision."

187

Types of Investors

Craig paused long enough to take from his glass of water before saying "There is quite a bit to learn about each different investment type. Investing can be a big scary venture for those who know little or nothing about it. Fortunately, the amount of information that you need to learn has a direct relation to the type of investor that you are. There are basically three types of investors: conservative, moderate, and aggressive. The different types of investments also cater to the two levels of risk tolerance as I have mention earlier.

"**Conservative investors** often invest in cash. This means that they put their money in interest bearing savings accounts, money market accounts, mutual funds, Gilts or the US Treasury bills, and Certificates of Deposit (CD). These are very safe investments that grow over a long period of time. These are also low risk investments.

"**Moderate investors** often invest in cash and bonds, and may dabble in the stock market. Moderate investing may be low or moderate risks. Moderate investors often also invest in real estate, providing that it is low risk real estate.

"**Aggressive investors** commonly do most of their investing in the stock market, which is higher risk. They also tend to invest in business ventures as well as higher risk real estate. For instance, if an aggressive investor puts his or her money into an older apartment building, then invests more money renovating the property, they are running a risk. They expect to be able to rent the apartments out for more money than the apartments are currently worth – or to sell the entire property for a profit on their initial investments. In some cases, this works out just fine, and in other cases, it doesn't. It's a risk. So I must give you a word of caution here:

- Before you start investing, it is very important that you learn about the different types of investments, and what those investments can do for you.

- Understand the risks involved, and pay attention to past trends as well. History does indeed repeat itself, and investors know this first hand!

"Would you say I summed it up nicely Madam?", Craig asked, directing his gaze at Helena Goldsmith.

"I couldn't have said it better myself" Mrs Goldsmith replied, scarcely holding back her high regard for this *new* Craig.

"Thank you Madam", Craig said smiling.

The Importance of Diversification

"I can consider myself a Moderate Investor" Helena said after a few moments. "Maybe it is because my risk tolerance is not very high but I have learnt that when it comes to investing, diversification is the key to success.

"You've probably heard the saying '**don't put all of your eggs in one basket!**' over and over again in your lives; it is very true. All successful investors build portfolios that are widely diversified, and you should too!

> Give a portion to seven, and also to eight; for you know not what evil shall be upon the earth.
> Ecclesiastes 11:2 (The Bible)

"Diversifying your investments might include purchasing various stocks in many different industries. It may include purchasing bonds, investing in money market accounts, or even in some real estate properties. The key is to invest in several different areas – not just one.

"Over time, research has shown that investors who have diversified portfolios usually see more consistent and stable returns on their investments than those who just invest in just one thing. By investing in several different markets, you will actually be at less risk also.

"For instance, if you have invested all of your money in one stock, and that stock takes a significant plunge, you will most likely find that you have lost all of your money. On the other hand, if you have invested in ten different stocks, and nine are doing well while one plunges, you are still in reasonably good shape. This is referred to as *Horizontal Diversification*.

"A good diversification will usually include stocks, bonds, real estate properties, and cash. This is referred to as *Vertical Diversification*. It may take time to diversify your portfolio. Depending on how much you have to initially invest, you may have to start with one type of investment, and invest in other areas as time goes on. This is fine, but if you can divide your initial investment funds among various types of investments, you will find that you have a lower risk of losing your money, and over time, you will see better returns."

"Mum, I must say I am surprised at how much you know about investing" Jennifer said, speaking for the first time in almost one hour!

"I'm glad you're here today Mrs Goldsmith, I couldn't have imagined this session being so interesting" Craig said in appreciation of Helena's contributions.

"You two will make a good tag-team on investments; judging from the way you kept taking turns during this session" Desmond jested but in admiration of his friend and his mother-in-law.

Investing Mistakes to Avoid

Craig looked around and noticed that everyone seemed to be quite satisfied with what they'd gained during the session, so he decided to round up.

"We've covered quite a lot today but I still have one final aspect that I think we need to touch." Craig announced to gain everybody's attention once again.

"It is possible that along the way you may, like I did, make a few investing mistakes, however there are big mistakes that you absolutely must avoid if you are to be a successful investor. We've already touched some of them but allow me just re-iterate as it is necessary. For instance, the biggest investing mistake that you could ever make is to not invest at all, or to put off investing until later. Start early to make your money work for you – even if all you can spare is £50 a month to invest!

"While not investing at all or putting off investing until later are big mistakes, investing before you are in the financial position to do so is equally a big mistake. Get your current financial situation in order first, and then start investing. Get your credit cleaned up, pay off high interest loans and credit cards, and put at least three months of living expenses aside for emergencies. Once these are accomplished, you are ready to begin making your money work for you full-time.

"Don't invest to get rich quick. That is the riskiest type of investing that there is, and you will more than likely lose. If it was easy, everyone would be doing it! Instead, invest for the long term and have the patience to weather the storms and allow your money to grow. Only invest for the short term when you know you will need the money in a short amount of time, and then stick with *safe* investments, such as certificates of deposit.

"Don't put all of your eggs into one basket. Scatter them around various types of investments for the best returns. Also, don't move your money around too much. Let it ride. Pick your investments carefully, invest your money, and allow it to grow – don't panic if the stock drops a few pounds. If the stock is a stable stock, it will go back up.

"A common mistake that a lot of people make is to think that their investments in collectibles like coins, stamps etc will really pay off. Again, if this were true, everyone would do it. Don't count on your Coke bottle-top collection or your book collection to pay for your retirement years! Count on investments made with cold hard cash instead."

"With God on our side and you just a phone call away, we will definitely avoid these mistakes" Desmond declared, patting his friend on the back.

Milestone #9

Teach Your Children about Money

Chapter 14

Passing the Financial 'Baton' to the Next Generation

It was supposed to be a quiet Friday evening visit to the Ellmases (and Jennifer of course); or so Craig thought. Sally had planned the kind of Friday-Night-In which they used to have when they were Undergraduates at the University of Greenwich. The sort of night with movies, pizza, popcorn, soft drinks, one *impromptu* discussion or two and generally lazing around until the early hours of the morning.

That was until Mr & Mrs Ellmas (Senior), Desmond's parents, showed up to pick the children, Felicia and Freda, for the weekend even though they had them the previous weekend.

Pa Ellmas and Ma Ellmas' arrival was accompanied by the usual enthusiastic screams of their grand-daughters who were yet to finish packing their 'stuff' for the weekend. After all the hugging, kissing and handshaking had been completed, the elderly Ellmases settled down in the living room to wait for the girls to finish packing.

"I see you've turned out as well as I've always thought you will" Pa Ellmas began, looking in his usual 'you-can't-hide-anything-from-me' way at Craig.

"I'm just managing sir" Craig answered while quickly thinking of what he can say to deflect the conversation away from himself.

"That's not what I heard. Apart from you owning your own businesses, Desmond even informed me that you were the one who's been helping them get out of their tough financial situation" Pa Ellmas pressed in.

"Oh no Pa Ellmas, Desmond and Sally did all the work; I just gave them advice."

"Don't be so modest my boy. You taught them from your own experience; you can't put a value to that" the elderly man said. "A man with experience is never at the mercy of a man who only has opinions. Think about that."

Pa Ellmas' last statement brought a big smile to Craig's face at the sight of which the elderly man turned to his wife with all seriousness and said "I taught that boy ALL he knows" directing his thumb towards Craig.

"You did?" Ma Ellmas asked both in surprise and amusement. "When was that?"

"The time he used to come to MY house to eat MY food, mess up MY house and make terrible noise with those excuses for guitar-playing."

"Those were the days Dad" Desmond said with a large grin on his face.

"I'm just glad your friend was listening to me - even back then" Pa Ellmas told his son.

"If you truly, truly (and I know it is not true) taught Craig all he knows, why didn't you teach our son as well?" Ma Ellmas asked setting a trap to catch her husband in.

Realising that all eyes were on him, Pa Ellmas pushed out his chest, touched the side of his nose with his forefinger and said quietly "I had a plan all along"

"What was the plan, sir?" asked Jennifer who had then re-entered the living room after helping her nieces pack while Sally attended to her in-laws.

"I knew if I taught Craig about money, he will in turn pass on the knowledge to this 'knuckle-head' (Desmond) here when the time comes. You know - like Paul said in 2nd Timothy 2:2" Pa Ellmas answered. "From the look of things, my plan worked".

> **"And the things that thou hast heard of me among many witnesses, the same commit thou to faithful men, who shall be able to teach others also."**
> 2nd Timothy 2:2 (The Bible)

"Yeah, right. The Bible says 'among many witnesses'. Where are your witnesses?" Ma Ellmas asked him as she headed towards the girls' room while everyone else laughed.

Just then, the picture of the winner of a well-publicised lottery jackpot came up on the television. Sally increased the volume when she realised everyone seemed interested in knowing what was being said about the man. The newscaster informed viewers that the 36-years-old man, who won over £9.2million less than 4 years ago, has just been declared bankrupt. This brought a big "whoa" from everyone in the room.

"How can you spend £9.2million in 4 years?" Pa Ellmas asked "I don't seem to understand how you young people think these days."

"Without being sensible financially, anybody can do what that man did. Who knows, we too may have blown the whole amount if we had £9.2million five years ago" Sally informed everyone.

"You are quite right Sally" Desmond agreed "At the rate at which we were going, bankruptcy would have come sooner than that for us."

"You two seem to have learnt your lesson now; thank God. Let's just hope your daughters haven't picked up on your old financial habits" Pa Ellmas said, raising his hands to heaven as if in prayers.

"I know of some people who have lost more money than that after winning the lottery" Jennifer ventured into the conversation.

"Let's leave the lottery discussion for another day because losing your jackpot winnings are not the only ways people show their financial incompetence these days" Craig finally joined in now since he was no longer the topic of the discussion. "We have heard stories of people who inherited large sums of money from their parents or other wealthy relatives only to squander the whole lot within eighteen months."

"Mind you, the inheritance Craig is talking about here usually takes an average person some forty odd years to accumulate during his or her lifetime ... and someone blows the lot in eighteen months! Can you imagine that?" Pa Ellmas interjected.

"You are very correct sir" Craig complemented the old man. "Most of the time, as you all probably know, there would have been little or no training in money management for these people. None of us here, by the way, sat through a 'Money Management 101' course in school or college ‑ so you might as well forget about our educational system providing you with any money management skills.

"But *we* have been going through that kind of a class with you for many months now, haven't we?" Sally reminded him

"Yes, and you are blessed. I had to go through the school of hard-knocks to learn what I know now; coupled, of course, with what Pa Ellmas 'taught' me."

"Now you're talking" Pa Ellmas said, loving the reference to his 'contribution'.

"So ... what has he been doing before now? Singing...? Eh?" Ma Ellmas asked her husband from the kitchen doorway.

The ensuing laughter gave Craig a few seconds to collect his thoughts a bit before continuing.

"The Bible talks more about finances than most Christians think. Over 2350 of its verses deal with how we should earn, give, save, spend, invest and distribute money (if I haven't missed anything out). That is more than the verses on both faith and prayer put together"

"Preach it Brother, preach it" Desmond jested.

"Thank you, thank you my Brother" Craig responded before continuing.

"Majority of the populace is not as blessed as we are, for the reason that they pick up what they know about finances literally on the streets; most of which are the wrong materials anyway. They learn and believe myths instead of truths. Home, in my opinion, is the first place where people should learn about money management and it should form a large part of home training for children."

"What if the child is not so inclined?" Pa Ellmas asked. "The only trait of money management skills that Desmond showed as a child was just to demand for and spend money."

"My sister was a bit like that when we were younger; but she could also make money from any item or event" Sally added, earning herself a little elbow jab from Jennifer.

"This one is for these young people here, Pa Ellmas" Craig said, looking at the only grandfather in their midst. "I know I'm not a parent yet but I'll like to share with you how I think you can pass your legacy and wisdom of managing your finances on to your children."

"I like the word 'yet' that you just used. You and Jenny should just make up your minds, get married and start making babies" Sally said, causing everyone to burst out laughing.

"I knew something was going on between those two" Pa Ellmas said to his wife, in not so low a tone.

"No you didn't, you've just been informed" Ma Ellmas replied out loud. "I hope you remember what the Bible says: 'you lie; you fry'."

"No it doesn't" responded Pa Ellmas, facing his wife squarely to the amusement of the younger generation. Sally, the usually cool-headed one, was laughing almost uncontrollably on the chair beside the elderly couple.

"Alright, alright, let me just continue so I can have time to talk with Jenny later" Craig said, even though feeling a bit embarrassed at becoming the topic of the discussion once again.

Use Responsibility to Teach Children Money Management

"Look people, the world out there is tough as we all know and it is getting tougher by the day. The sooner we start teaching our children about personal financial responsibility the better. Our children can begin learning the basics about money at a very early age.

"We may start when they are just about 3 years old. Take them to the supermarket or other stores where you shop and explain often and in many ways, that the money you (and your spouse) earn while you are away working is what pays for the food and other items that you are buying. Give the child a small amount of money, let him (or her) choose something he wants and pay for it himself (or herself).

"Begin giving the child a small, and I mean small, weekly allowance when he or she is about 6 or 7 years old. Get the child a piggy bank and teach him or her to tithe first, save second, spend third, ...and then with your guidance, of course, learn the reasons for doing them and to do them wisely. Let the allowance be paid on the same day every week. This will give the child a sense of knowing how long the 'spend' part of the allowance should last.

"Give the child small chores that he or she can easily manage and attach doing the chores to receiving the allowance. In other words, help him come to the obvious conclusion that work equals income. Do not hesitate to withhold the allowance if the chores are not done and let him suffer the consequences. Don't provide him with the ice cream cone that he would have bought with his allowance had he done the work.

"Pick a date, such as his birthday, to increase his allowance and the chores required of him.

201

"When the child is about 12 to 14 begin encouraging him or her to earn extra money by getting some jobs on his own...such as mowing the neighbours' lawns and, also, encourage him to save for things he would consider long term goals such as buying a games console or whatever else he or she may desire. By this time, the child should have moved from saving in a piggy-bank to a proper bank's savings account into which he can save himself but requires your permission to withdraw from.

"A part-time job should be considered by the time he is 16. Just be sure it's not one that will interfere with his school work. By the way, show your children respect for other people and their work. Be cordial to waiters, parking lot attendants, electricians – and everyone else whose services you require. If you don't, you are teaching your children to disrespect people and the value of the work they do.

"After the teenager completes his or her GCSE exams or graduates from high school and is ready to start college; if all the above have been followed, he or she should be ready to use a debit card with little supervision and make good choices in money management. If not, still let him get the debit card but add that you will deposit money to the account as required but, also, let him or her know that you will be able to see exactly how the money is being spent and that there are limits – no overdrafts.

"Truth be told; I think we did the best we could with you our children. By '*we*', I'm speaking for my generation okay?" Pa Ellmas said.

"Yes Pa Ellmas and we are grateful for that" Craig replied him. "But the rules of the credit and debt game have changed. We can't teach our children about money the same way you taught us.

"This is war and the enemy has changed both his weapons and his tactics. The debt-traps have juicier baits nowadays in the form of gifts and incentives to take credit cards; advertisers bombarding us through the airwaves and press with almost constant appeal to buy, buy and then buy some more.

"Proverbs 22:6-7 gives the best instruction on this matter. We are to give our children training so they won't go into the financial slavery that we have now been delivered from."

> "Train up a child in the way he should go: and when he is old, he will not depart from it. The rich rule over the poor and the borrower is servant to the lender."
> Proverbs 22:6-7 (The Bible)

"Craig, you should be a preacher" Ma Ellmas said when Craig stopped talking.

"That's what I have been saying all along" added Pa Ellmas

"Oh here we go again" Ma Ellmas said rising up from her seat. Calling out to get her grandchildren she asked "Girls are you ready now?"

"Yes Grandma" was the chorused reply as the girls, now ten years old, came into the room with their backpacks.

"Well that's my cue" Pa Ellmas said signalling to Desmond to help him up from his seat. "We have to be running along now."

With everyone now on their feet, Pa Ellmas placed one hand on Craig's shoulder and said "I'm proud of you my boy and I know your father, God rest his soul, would have been proud too".

Then lowering his voice and pulling Craig closer to him, he said "What's the deal with our lady friend here?" referring to Jennifer.

"We are just good friends sir" Craig replied.

"Good friends my foot. I have eyes you know", the older man said. "If you've prayed and feel the leading of God, make the move; say something and stop behaving like a schoolboy."

Craig could only nod in response.

"Stop wasting time..." Pa Ellmas added as he finally released Craig "... and give our love to your Mama" to the hearing of others.

"The Taxi's here" Sally called out.

As they all headed for the front door, Desmond said to his father "Are you sure you don't want me to drop you at home?"

"Yes I'm sure. You stay with your people here; we have our granddaughters" Pa Ellmas replied him patting him on the back.

After saying goodbye to her children and her in-laws, Sally turned to Jennifer and asked "What did she say to you Jenny?"

"Who?", Jennifer asked.

"Ma Ellmas."

"Oh she said 'that's a fine young man' referring to Craig I think" Jennifer answered.

"They've known Craig even before Desmond and I started dating. Their house was like a second home for Craig; so she should know - just like I do" Sally explained with all seriousness.

"Well, we shall see" Jennifer said shrugging her shoulders.

By the time the ladies re-joined the Craig and Desmond, the living room had been transformed. The centre-table has been moved away from its usual position and was cover with all sorts of soft drinks; sweets, popcorn bowls etc.

"I guess that's the lot" Desmond said surveying his work around the room.

As if on cue, the doorbell rang. "That's the pizza" Craig said, as he got up to answer the door. "Now let the movie-night begin."

"I'm glad the children are not here to see all the unhealthy food items we have to eat tonight" Sally said, shaking her head.

"That's part of what you should NOT be teaching them" Craig said to her.

"Come on, sit down and let's all share the 'blame', caffeine, cholesterol and the fat" Desmond said to Sally, patting the seat beside him.

"So what movie are we watching first?" Craig asked, carefully balancing himself on the carpet within reach of both the popcorn and the pizza.

"*Madea Goes to Jail!*" chorused the ladies, referring to Tyler Perry's play.

Milestone #10

Attain Financial Freedom

&

Leave A Legacy

Chapter 15

Habits of the Financially-Smart

Desmond and Sally Ellmas have, for the past forty-four months, had their friend Craig Lamu as their financial coach. With his help, they have been able to move from being deeply in debt to now being well on their way to financial freedom.

The Ellmases no longer had any credit card or consumer loan debt. At the rate at which they were going their mortgage would be completely paid off in another forty-five months. They had almost five complete months of emergency fund saved away – for the rainy-day and they were still adding a small portion of their disposable income to it every month. They were joyfully paying their tithe which is 10% of their income; they were investing another 10% for retirement while yet another 10% is being saved for purposes such as their children's university education, a new kitchen etc. They even started an internet business from it about 11 months ago.

Today had been earmarked as the final session with Craig; and his friends were expecting him to make a big 'graduation' speech but they were not prepared for what he had in mind for them.

Craig arrived on time and as usual looking well-dressed for the occasion. This session, the Ellmases knew, could not be a long one because Craig would be going out on a lunch date with Jennifer in the next two hours. Things had been going on so well between those two that Sally was already wishing Craig would just step up to the next level with the relationship. Craig made himself comfortable at his, now favourite, corner of the living room where he could see most of what is going on in the room as well as the kitchen area.

After Desmond and Sally were seated also, Craig began the 'speech'.

"Just under four years guys and look at what you have done for yourselves; see how far you've come." he began.

"We owe it all to you" Sally said trying to give him praise. "If you hadn't come in when you did, who knows what would have happened to us by now"

"Oh no, I won't take that at all. All glory and praise belong to God. He was the one that saw me through my own journey to financial freedom after I became so broke that I couldn't even pay attention!!" At this, everyone laughed. At that moment Jennifer walked into the room; she looked around at everyone in amusement wondering what was so funny.

"We........" Craig attempted to continue just before he saw Jennifer walk into the room.

Jennifer was naturally beautiful and she had the gift of knowing how to use makeup properly. With or without it, her stunning appearance almost always turns every head in any gathering she goes to. Today she even looked more gorgeous than ever in her simple v-neck, flower-patterned, cotton blouse on a figure-hugging, blue jeans trousers; almost matching in simplicity what Craig, the 'Mr-Easy-Like-A-Sunday-Morning' was wearing.

For a moment, Craig was lost for words; his eyes became as big as saucers at the sight of this creation of God standing before him. Deep down, he was thanking God for creating a woman like Jennifer and sending her into his world.

Before Jennifer sat down beside Sally, she looked straight at Craig and asked "what do you think?" referring to her outfit.

"Em... em... the truth is ... I... I... I can't think right now" Craig replied her without blinking an eye. This drew another round of laughter from the Ellmases.

Lifestyle Creep

Craig used the laughter and the look of satisfaction on Jennifer's face to recover. Then he continued his 'speech'.

"Let me get back to what I was saying before I was pleasantly interrupted by *Her Gorgeousness*" Craig continued, bringing a big smile to Jennifer's face; making her look even more beautiful.

"Well Sally and Desmond, you guys have done it. You are more than halfway to your financial freedom. To reach this stage, you have had to change some of your financial habits. For example, from the 'buy, buy, buy' and 'spend, spend, spend' habits, you changed to the 'pay-off, pay-off, pay-off' and 'save, save, save' habits.

"Now you have added habit of invest, invest, and invest some more to your 'portfolio'. You need to keep this one going until you become totally, financially free and beyond. As we have discussed earlier, your investment strategy depends on your ages, family situation, goals, disposable income etc; It is not a one-size-fits-all thing.

"We know, Craig; but why do you have to say every word three times?" Desmond asked.

211

"To be sure you remember; morning, noon and night" Jennifer replied him.

"So you are taking his side now, huh?" Desmond said

"Look Craig, don't mind these two. Please just go on" Sally said, playfully pulling her husband's ear.

"It's okay Sally. I'm trying to make sure you don't make the same mistake that I almost made at this stage of the game. Don't fall victims to Lifestyle Creep" Craig said, emphasising the last two words knowing the term would get everybody's attention. He was right.

"Lifestyle Creep?" Sally repeated. "What's that?"

"A 'creepy' new term created to show us that we haven't 'arrived' yet. Am I right?" Desmond ventured without trying to completely disguise his ignorance of the term.

"Not entirely but you are not far from the truth either" Craig said encouraging him.

"Lifestyle Creep is a situation where people's lifestyle or standard of living improves as their discretionary income rises either through an increase in income or decrease in expenses. As lifestyle creep occurs, and more money is spent on lifestyle, former luxuries are now considered necessities.

"According to my friends at *Investopedia*, 'Lifestyle creep is particularly a problem to those individuals approaching retirement. People who are five to ten years to retirement are typically in their peak earning years, but at the same time many of their earlier expenses, such as paying off a mortgage or raising a family have been reduced dramatically. Faced with a surplus of cash, some people use it to buy more expensive cars, more expensive vacations or possibly a second home'.

212

"Since the goal in retirement is to maintain the lifestyle enjoyed in the last few years before retirement, these retirees require more funds to support their new, more lavish lifestyles. Unfortunately, they don't have the resources to do this because they spent their surplus cash flow instead of investing it."

"Wow!" Desmond exclaimed. "How can we be sure that we haven't already started our own Lifestyle Creep?"

"You only have to check your Spending Plan again. Re-define your needs, wants and desires." Craig answered. "Be sure that your wants have not turned up on the Spending Plan as needs."

"Does it mean we can't even enjoy some luxury?" Sally asked this time with a little bit of concern in her voice.

"No, no, not at all", Craig replied quickly. "You should enjoy what you have worked for but not at the detriment of your retirement when you won't be able to work as hard or at all - anymore. Just check on your new habits from time to time and see what they will do to your retirement.

"Okay people; I think this has actually ushered us nicely into today's session. You see, we humans are creatures of habits. Some of our habits actually save us time, they are skills we learnt a long time ago; yet we still use them to go about our lives, work, business etc. In a nutshell habits save us time and energy to get things done like our writing and reading abilities, how you tie your shoe laces, how to drive your car and how to cook. Some habits are good but yet there are other habits that aren't in our best interest.

"The most significant consequence of NOT making something a habit is that these activities would stand a good chance of not getting done, either because we forgot about them or because, even having remembered, we lack the ability to motivate ourselves at the time of the remembering to take any action. It takes energy to remember and then motivate a new action. Habituated actions are far less energy consuming."

"I totally agree" Desmond said, breaking the monologue.

"Agreeing with me alone will not get the job done; you need to make these habits you'll be learning about YOUR habits as well", Craig said leaning towards his best friend. "If you have good habits, financial or otherwise, there won't be room for you to develop the bad ones. To be financially-free, you have to think like the financially-free, behave like the financially-free, and have the habits of the financially-free."

With his 'speech' finished, Craig reached for the folder he brought and removed some sheets of paper.

"There's more?" Desmond asked in astonishment.

"If you start reading those now, you'll be late for your lunch" Sally reminded Craig (and Jennifer).

"Oh no, I'm not reading these. You are." Craig said, handing the papers to Desmond who sat closest to him.

"Over the years, I have studied some activities consistently carried out by people who eventually became financially-free; these same activities, I have also noticed, are only occasionally carried out by most other people; which led me to document them for use by the people I coach in financial matters.

"Here they are for you to read and follow. I'm off to lunch. Are you ready Jennifer?" Craig asked standing up.

"Yes Craig, you lead the way" Jennifer answered standing at the same time as her sister. "Where are we going?"

"It's a surprise" Craig said, taking her hand as they headed for the door.

Desmond looked through the papers and to himself he started to read:

Develop the mind-set of the financially-smart

1. Keep in mind that a habit is a recurrent, often unconscious pattern of behaviour that is acquired through repetition. **Cultivate good, money-saving and wealth-building habits**. Be conscious of what you spend time on daily.

2. To permanently change the temperature of a room, you need to reset the thermostat. In the same way, your financial 'thermostat' needs to be reset for you to achieve financial freedom. **Be conscious of how you think about money**.

3. **Decide that NOW is the time to take action**. Your FUTURE is determined by what you do TODAY. The difference, between achievers and non-achievers, is not just knowledge, *it is action*

4. **Change the way you think about money**. The reason a vast majority of people never accumulate a substantial nest egg is because they don't understand the nature of money or how it works.

5. Even if you don't agree, **blame NOBODY for your current financial situation**. Use your energy to *take the bull by the horns* and become free.

6. **Visualise yourself financially-free** and aim at it. What you see is what you get.

215

7. **Aim higher than you've ever done**. If you include the success of others with yours, you might just get it.

8. **Follow your passion**. You are much more likely to become rich by doing something you are passionate about and can get paid for.

9. **Never stop learning**. Learn something new each day no matter how small.

> "If a man empties his purse into his head, no one can take it away from him. An investment in knowledge always pays the best interest"
> - Benjamin Franklin

10. Read at least one book, magazine on money or finances every month.

11. **Study after successful people**. A very wise investor once said to pick the traits you admire and dislike the most about your heroes, then do everything in your power to develop the traits you like and reject the ones you don't.

12. **Invest early and let compound interest take care of all of the work**. With your advice and the help, your children too can live comfortably knowing their future will be free of money worries.

13. **Unless your parents were wealthy, don't do what they did.** The definition of insanity is doing the same thing over and over again and expecting a different result. You must break away from the mentality of past generations if you want to have a different lifestyle than they had.

14. **More money in itself is not the answer.** More money is not going to solve your problem. Money is like a magnifying glass; it will accentuate and bring to light your true habits and character.

Get organised in readiness for freedom

15. **Set goals.** Make sure they are specific, measurable, achievable, relevant and time-bound.

16. **Write down your goals** as this crystallises your thinking and may push you to action.

17. **Identify your goals clearly and why they matter to you,** and decide which are most important. By concentrating your efforts, you have a better chance of achieving what matters most.

18. **Focus first on the goals that matter.** To accomplish primary goals, you will often need to put desirable but less important ones on the back burner.

19. Remember that computers crash. **Back up all your critical information regularly** in at least two different locations of your choice.

20. **Regularly check your credit reports** from the relevant organisations. It's the best way to avoid identity theft and catch reporting errors as soon as they occur.

Understand how money works

21. **Invest.** Make your money work for you instead of working for money all your life.

22. **Rule of 72**. Dividing 72 by the interest you receive on an investment calculates how long it will take to double your investment without adding anymore savings.

23. **Tap into the power of compound interest**. If a 20-year-old invests just £100 a month and gains 10% annually, he or she will be a millionaire by the age of 65 – even though he or she only saved a total of just over £54,000.

24. **Develop an understanding of the power of small amounts**. Don't suffer from the "not enough" mentality; with the little you have, start saving and then investing. A big portfolio is built £1 at a time.

25. **Budgets are a necessary evil**. They are the best practical ways to get a grip on your spending -- and to make sure your money is being used the way you want it to be used. No matter how much you make you need a budget.

26. **Create a Net Worth Statement**. Add the current value of everything you own and subtract the total value of everything you owe.

27. **Track and revise your Net Worth** Statement each quarter. What you track will increase; this is the law of focus.

Cultivate healthy financial habits

28. Be aware that there are two types of habits – the 'doing' habits and the 'not doing' habits. We all have both but we need to know whether they are helping or hurting us.

29. **Schedule meetings with your family to discuss finances**. Set up goals and a plan that the family can work on together.

30. **Nothing beats hard work**. Hard work is the habit first among equals. Achieving financial freedom is often the result of consistent diligence. We have all heard of individuals who found wealth through inheritance or the lottery, and then lose everything because they did not appreciate the wealth having not worked for it. The bible teaches us that: *'Hard work brings prosperity; playing around bring poverty'* (Proverbs 28:19 TLB).

31. **Pay yourself** as conscientiously as you have paid any lending institution. 10% of all your earnings must go into your future as passive or active investments.

32. **Automate your saving process**. Have your bank automatically transfer a set amount each month into your savings account.

33. **Have an 'Emergency Fund'**. Save enough cash to see you through at least three months of lean times. If you lose your job, you won't then have to use credit cards to pay for daily expenditures.

34. **Get Insured**. Given Murphy's Law, if you have insurance, you will never need it. If you don't, disaster will inevitably strike. You need to protect yourself, your family and your belongings.

35. **Live modestly**. Modest living can produce great wealth on a modest income. In contrast, frivolous uncontrolled spending can result in financial turmoil even for the highest paid among us.

36. **Spend less than you make**. If your outgo exceeds your income, your upkeep will be your downfall.

37. **Pay your bills on time** – integrity demands it. For recurring bills, schedule automatic payments through

your bank's online services so you will never miss a payment.

38. **Beware of spending creep**. As your annual income climbs from raises, promotions, and smart investing, don't start spending for luxuries until you are sure that you are staying ahead of inflation. It is better to use those income increases as excuses to save more.

39. **Pay for your credit card bills as soon as you receive them**. Don't just believe in doing so – do it. Remember: Earning 5% in your savings account doesn't mean much if you are paying 23% interest on unpaid card balances.

40. **Be patient**. Don't buy the latest new gadgets today. Even if you must get it, wait a few months for prices to come down and you are able.

41. **Return phone calls within a day**. If you can't manage that, return them the next day. Be organised, you need to be responsive; you never when an opportunity might show up.

42. **Be safe**. Shred all your financial statements, bills and credit cards before you dispose of them. Not all identity theft occurs online.

43. **Be sure to use your leisure time for leisure.** But don't use your work time for leisure. Use work time for work.

44. When you finish work, **make your agenda for the following day**. This saves time; the ideas are in your mind, and the next morning you can review, prioritise and get started immediately. It's a jump-start on your day.

45. **Pay attention to your moods.** When you feel motivated, use that energy to get a project done. Don't waste your best time on leisure, use it for accomplishment.

46. **Talk yourself into financial freedom.** Banish the word "expensive" from your vocabulary. Replace it with, "That's not a priority for me right now." Banish the sentence "I can't afford it." Replace it with, "That's on my wish list."

47. **Stop talking about what you don't have.** Replace it with appreciation for what you have and enjoy now.

48. **Pray.** God knows what you cannot even think of. Ask Him for wisdom.

49. **Never burn bridges.** If you happen to leave your current employment, leave on good terms. This will put you in a good light with your former management and can result in a good reference, another job, a consultancy role etc... Never leave on bad terms.

50. **Be generous.** Even before you've *made it*, cultivate the habit of helping others less fortunate than yourself. Regardless of your beliefs when you donate time and money to help others you will inadvertently help yourself. You will feel great too.

Play the credit 'game' like a Pro

51. **Deal with debt.** Increase the payments being made to creditors as much as you possible can.

52. Transfer credit card balances to cards with special zero or low-interest introductory offers – and pay off the balances while those low rates are in force!!!

53. Eliminate credit card debt to increase your income with no additional effort.

54. Pay off your card balances each month if you have to use your credit card.

55. **Reduce the Interest rate**. Phone with the credit card companies see if they'll reduce the interest rate on your accounts. It's worth a try, and if they say no, you haven't lost anything.

56. Look for competitive credit card interest rates to transfer to.

57. Keep a record of any telephone credit card transactions and keep receipts until the statement comes in

58. Be aware of your credit limit and don't go beyond it. Be aware of your credit limit, consider a personal loan if you are carrying a balance regularly.

59. **NEVER use credit cards for cash advances**. The interest rates are outrageous.

Invest wisely

60. **Invest your time before you invest your money**. Read books, newspaper articles and magazines on investment.

61. **Prepare your mind-set.** Invest wisely and not emotionally. Invest using your extra money, money that you don't need in the short term.

62. **Set your investment objective**.
    Do you want to:
    - **a.** preserve your capital;
    - **b.** generate income; or
    - **c.** grow the value of your holdings?

In general, those are the three main objectives that you can reach by investing.

63. **Invest for the long-term**. Over the long term, stocks have historically outperformed all other investments.

64. Over the short term, stocks can be hazardous to your financial health.

65. Don't invest heavily until you have a cash reserve that can prevent you from having to liquidate your investments if you suffer a financial setback.

66. Never invest more than 10% of your stock portfolio in any one company, even if everyone says it is a "sure thing."

67. If you don't understand how an investment works, don't buy it.

68. Spread your money among a number of different types of investments. A diversified portfolio is less risky than a portfolio that is concentrated in one or a few investments.

Be cautious of the 'Taxman'

69. Maintain well-organised records of all your expenses and income. The tax filing will not scare you if you have your paperwork organised.

70. Get more from your depreciation. Take the extra trouble at tax time to list items on a property—from air conditioning to light fixtures—as personal property. As personal property, items can be depreciated over shorter useful lives.

Teach your children about money

71. **Give your kids a rewards for chores done**, so they will learn to tie the spending of a given sum to work completed (if an allowance, to a finite period of time). This is called budgeting.

72. **Let your children work**. The best way they can learn to truly appreciate money is to earn it for themselves.

73. **Show respect for people who serve you in any way**. Be cordial to waiters, parking lot attendants, electricians etc. – and everyone else whose services you require. If you don't, you are teaching your children to disrespect people and the value of the work they do.

74. **When it is time to buy clothes** for the school year, give your children a specific amount of money and **let them do their own shopping**. You will be surprised at how quickly they find their way to the sales section.

75. **Start saving early for college**. Tertiary education costs are rising at the rate of about 5% annually, so start today to keep pace.

76. If your children are not sure what they want to do after graduation, encourage them to take time off to work while they think about it. It's cheaper to be indecisive while they're working.

77. **Encourage your children to start a company while still in college**. The business faculty and successful alumni can offer high-grade advice at no charge – and your young entrepreneur will graduate with a business underway.

Have multiple streams of income

78. **Don't depend only on your job;** find other businesses that can bring money on the side.

79. **Do the math.** When buying a house to renovate and sell, deduct the cost of your renovations from its fair market value. That's how much you should pay, not one penny more.

80. **Don't fall victim to analysis paralysis.** If you don't make offers, you won't buy property.

81. **The 'rat race' does not favour you.** Even if you win the 'rat race', you are still a rat. Think of ways to become your own boss.

82. **Prepare to stop working for other people.** All the world's billionaires have one thing in common. At some point, they stopped working for other people and started working for themselves.

83. **Start a business that lets you do what you love.** You will always do better in the business that is right for you, even though other enterprises might look more profitable.

84. When you work at home, it's easy to get off schedule because of interruptions or the temptation to take time off for leisure activities. Keep in mind that every moment wasted today usually means more work the next day.

85. **Don't allow personal tasks to get in the way of work.** These can be anything from cleaning the house to visits from friends or relatives to watching television. Take breaks from your computer, but try to avoid getting involved in personal tasks during those breaks.

86. **Take a marketing course before you start your business**, to learn how to kick start profits without hiring a costly sales force.

87. **Consider buying a business instead of starting one from scratch.** You can look at the books of a business that is for sale, identify improvements you can make – and have an operating business at a far lower cost.

Wisely pass your wealth to your heirs

88. **Don't wait to start estate planning**. The earlier you plan; the more opportunities you have to structure your estate wisely.

89. **Write a Will!** Some people believe that, if they don't have one, they will live forever. Sadly, it doesn't work that way.

90. **Review your Will every two years or so with your lawyer.** Changing circumstances in your life, as well as new laws, may necessitate its revisions.

91. If you can afford good old "fish n chips" or a burger every day, you can afford life insurance. Life insurance is essential for anyone who has dependants.

92. **Don't overbuy life insurance**. Carrying costly insurance to make your family rich when you die can make you poor while you are living.

93. If you plan to stay single with no dependants, you do not need life assurance against dying, but **you do need disability assurance** in case you become ill or are injured in an accident.

94. Have enough life insurance to replace at least five years of your salary or 10 years if you have younger kids or significant debts.

95. As you get older, reduce your term life insurance and let your heirs plan to get their inheritance from your investments and other sources. Term life insurance gets more expensive as you age.

96. If your heirs are looking forward to getting large insurance payments after you die, invite them to help you pay for your policies while you are still alive. Tell them it is a good investment.

Prepare Early for Good Retirement

97. **Change how you identify retirement.** Consider retirement as a new beginning, not end.

98. **Create an identity outside the workplace.** Start a hobby or other interests not related to work.

99. **Prepare now to retire comfortably later.** Approximately 80% of millionaires in the western world are first generation millionaires. Most earned their wealth through their own initiative and sound financial habits.

100. **Focusing on your retirement goal.** Always remind yourself that one of the reasons why you have to work, save and invest hard now is so you can have a worry-free and prosperous future!

101. **Don't buy a retirement house that is too big because you are expecting your kids or grandchildren to visit.** Buying a huge house for occasional visits is a common mistake made by many retirees. Inflatable or sofa beds are cheaper than additional rooms.

While Desmond was engrossed in reading the 'Habits of the Financially-Samrt', Sally escorted Craig and Jennifer to the door where she asked them about their plans for the afternoon.

"That's for us to know and for you to find out – later" Craig answered her. "After lunch, maybe we'll catch a movie."

"... Or two" Jennifer added.

"... And then go for a walk and later dinner" Craig said keeping the tease going.

"... Maybe have a coffee or two after that" Jennifer said hugging her sister.

"Thank you for everything Craig" Sally said as she hugged him.

"You're welcome; but the pleasure is all mine" Craig said, winking at Sally. "Actually you did ALL the work, I just guided you."

With that Craig took Jennifer's hand as they walked towards his car. His free hand instinctive went into his coat pocket just to make sure that the little box containing the ring was still there. He needed to 'pop the question' before the day was over.

"Have fun. I'll see you later" Sally said as she closed the door behind them to join her husband where he was still reading his new habits-to-be.

Chapter 16

What happens now?

Now that you know the habits of the financially-smart, it's time to get tactical. There are a number of activities you need to perform on the road to Financial Freedom. Seeing the **Milestones of Financial Freedom** along your way will at least give you the assurance that you are on the right path. They will take the frustration out of the whole exercise.

> **"Wealth is the slave of a wise man.**
> **The master of a fool."**
>
> - Seneca

By following these Milestones, you will not only become debt-free, but by creating other revenue sources apart from your job, you will eventually become financially-free. In fact, the more income avenues you have, the more the revenue you can generate and the wealthier you will become. You will then have many assets which will begin to feed you instead of the liabilities which used to eat you up.

When all is said and done, whatever you use your wealth for is what you will be remembered by. What do you want your life to account for? When you depart from this world, what legacy will you leave behind? If you remember that it is the Lord God Who has given you power to make wealth, when you actually make it, you will use the wealth for His glory. *"To whom much is given, much is expected"* - Luke 12:48

> **"Everything you receive from God is given to you in trust - including your life."**
>
> - Richard Jama

I hope I have generated enough excitement for freedom in you by now. If so, let's get you started down your road to financial freedom:

Milestone 1:
Create a Spending Plan

Milestone 2:
Save £1000 for Emergencies

Milestone 3:
Pay Off Credit Cards

Milestone 4:
Increase Emergency Fund to One Month's Living Expenses

Milestone 5:
Pay Off All Consumer Debt

Milestone 6:
Increase Emergency Fund to Three Months' Living Expenses

Milestone 7:
Pay Off Home Mortgage & Save for Major Expenses

Milestone 8:
Invest for Retirement

Milestone 9:
Teach Your Children about Money

Milestone 10:
Attain Financial Freedom & Leave a Legacy

Appendix A

Life/Financial Purpose and Goals

Date:

Short Term Goals

	Goal	Cost (£)	Time Frame	Per month
1				
2				
3				

Long Term Goals

	Goal	Cost(£)	Time Frame	Per month
1				
2				
3				

Monthly Savings Total

My special quotation or Bible verse:

Appendix B

DEBT TO INCOME RATIO CALCULATION	
MONTHLY DEBT PAYMENTS	
Monthly mortgage payment (include property/council taxes and insurance) or rent	£
Monthly home equity line of credit or loan payment	£
Monthly car payments	£
Monthly revolving credit payments (furniture, appliance loans, etc.)	£
Monthly student loan payments	£
Monthly minimum credit card payments	£
Other monthly loan amounts	£
Monthly child support payments	£
TOTAL MONTHLY DEBT PAYMENTS	£
MONTHLY INCOME	
Monthly NET (take-home) pay	£
Annual bonuses and overtime, divided by 12	£
Other annual income, divided by 12	£
TOTAL MONTHLY INCOME	£
DEBT TO INCOME RATIO	
Total Monthly Debt Payments Divided by Total Monthly Income = Debt to Income Ratio	%

Appendix C

Daily Spending Diary

Date	Item	Category	Cost
Total			

Appendix D

A	Fixed Costs	£
	Home	
	Mortgage / Rent	
	Electricity	
	Gas	
	Water Rate	
	Council Tax Payment	
	Building Insurance	
	Home Content Insurance	
	Transport	
	Car Loan Payment	
	Petrol	
	Commuting costs (travel card etc)	
	Car repairs, servicing, MOT etc	
	Other monthly bills	
	Telephone (Fixed line & Mobile)	
	Childcare	
	Life Insurance	
	Other	
	Less-than-monthly expenses	
	Home repairs	
	Appliances	
	Other expenses	
	Food (at home)	
	Laundry, cleaning etc	
	Medical costs	
	Other	
B	**Discretionary Spending**	£
	Food & Drink	
	Takeaways	
	Meal at restaurants	
	Entertainment	
	TV subscriptions	
	Books, magazines, newspapers	
	Other outings	
	Around the home	
	Home decorating	
	Gardening	
	Less-than-monthly expenses	
	Holiday, Travel	
	Birthdays, Christmas etc	
	Other Expenses	
	Total	

Glossary

Annual Equivalent Rate (AER) - a notional rate that illustrates what the annual rate of interest would be if the interest was compounded each time it was paid. Where interest is paid annually, the quoted rate and the AER are the same.

Annual Percentage Rate (APR) - It's the percentage rate which your loan will cost you each year, including all charges.

Appreciation - Increase in the price (or value) of a share or other asset. Appreciation is one component of total return. Payment of an income, in the form, say, of a dividend, is another.

Arrears - Amount overdue as a result of being behind payments.

Asset - Something that has earning potential or value.

Attachment of Earnings - This forces the debtor's employer to make deductions from the debtor's earnings and pay them to the creditor.

Bailiffs - Bailiffs are officers of the court, who can in certain circumstances be used by creditors to enforce judgments by collecting debts and repossessing homes or goods.

Bankruptcy - Bankruptcy is legal procedure for dealing with debts when you cannot pay.

Budget - A document listing details of income and expenditure.

Budget Deficit - The amount on your budget by which your expenditure exceeds your income before allowing for offers of payment on non-priority debts.

Budget Surplus - The amount on your budget by which your income exceeds your expenditure before allowing for offers of payments on non-priority debts.

Budgeting - The process of managing outgoings so that they don't exceed income.

Building Society - A mutual organisation, owned by the people saving with it and borrowing from it. Increasing numbers have converted to banks in recent years, paying windfall profits to the owners.

Certificate of deposit (CD) - Also called a time deposit this is a certificate issued by a bank or thrift that indicates a specified sum of money has been deposited. A CD has a maturity date and a specified interest rate, and can be issued in any denomination. The duration can be up to five years.

Compound Interest - The investors' best friend. £100 invested in the stock market in 1918 would be worth around £1,000,000 today, according to calculations done by Barclays Capital, a London merchant bank.

Contractual Payment - Payment agreed in the original contract with the creditor.

County Court Claim - This secures the debt on your home usually with conditions concerning payments. A charging order has the effect of converting an unsecured debt into a secured one.

County Court Judgment (CCJ) - Gives details of the court's decision of a creditor's attempt to recover a debt in a civil court.

Credit Crunch - A sudden reduction in the general availability of loans (or credit), or a sudden increase in the cost of obtaining loans from the banks.

Credit Limit - The amount of credit that a financial institution extends to a client. Credit limit also refers to the maximum amount a credit card company will allow someone to borrow on a single card.

Credit Rating - A credit scoring system which gives points to items of information given on your application form when applying for credit.

Creditor - Someone to whom you owe money.

Debt Consolidation - This is taking a new loan and using the proceeds to pay off several smaller debts.

Debt Management Plan - This is a repayment scheme administered by a Consumer Credit Counselling Service for people unable to pay their creditors the full contractual payments.

Debtor - Someone who owes money.

Direct Debit - The account holder instructs the bank or building society to comply with requests from a third party to make a series of payments to them.

Dividend - A distribution from a company to a shareholder in the form of cash, shares, or other assets. The most common kind of dividend is a distribution of earnings.

Downshifting - Making major changes to one's lifestyle caused by accepting a reduced level of income.

Equity - The difference between the market value of your house and the amount outstanding on your mortgage.

Gilts - When the government needs to borrow money, it sells you these. They are government bonds and as a rule the interest is paid gross (i.e. free of tax). They are very safe and their US equivalent is the Treasury bill, or "T-Bill".

Gross - The payment of any form of income (interest or dividend payout) without the prior deduction of tax.

Hire Purchase - An agreement where goods are hired for an agreed period, at the end of which the hirer has the option to purchase.

House Poor - A situation that describes a person who spends a large proportion of his or her total income on home ownership, including mortgage payments, property taxes, maintenance and utilities. House poor individuals are short of cash for discretionary items and tend to have trouble meeting other financial obligations like vehicle payments.

Individual Retirement Account (IRA) - An investing tool used by individuals to earn and earmark funds for retirement savings. There are several types of IRAs: Traditional IRAs, Roth IRAs, SIMPLE IRAs and SEP IRAs.

Individual Savings Account (ISA): ISAs started in April 1999 and replaced PEPs and TESSAs. ISAs are schemes to protect your investments (shares, bonds, cash or insurance funds) from tax. They can be regarded as tax-free wrappers.

Individual Voluntary Arrangement (IVA) - A means of protecting yourself from your creditors by entering into a legally binding agreement supervised by an Insolvency Practitioner.

Inflation - A fall in the value of money.

Insurance - A contract (policy) in which an individual or entity receives financial protection or reimbursement against losses from an insurance company. The company pools clients' risks to make payments more affordable for the insured.

Irregular Bill - An occasional expense e.g. TV licence, car/road tax, birthdays etc.

Intestate - The act of dying without a legal Will. Determining the distribution of the deceased's assets then becomes the responsibility of a probate court.

Joint and Several liabilities - If two or more parties enter into a credit agreement they will each be liable for repaying the whole amount borrowed.

Late Fees - Fees added to the amount owed by the debtor when payments are late and where such fees are allowed for in the original contract.

Monthly Expenses - The amount of money needed each month to pay your rent or mortgage, your gas, electricity and water, your food and other living expenses.

Mortgage - A loan to buy a home, where you put up the property as a security against you paying back the loan. Mortgages offer by far the best long-term interest rates of any loan because they are the least risky of loans.

Mutual Fund - The US equivalent to UK's unit trust.

Negative Equity - When the value of an asset falls below the outstanding balance on the loan used to purchase that asset. Negative equity is calculated simply by taking the value of the asset less the balance on the outstanding loan.

Nest Egg - A special sum of money saved or invested for one specific future purpose.

Non-Priority Debts - Non-Priority Debts are those where the creditor cannot deprive you of liberty, home or essential goods and services.

Portfolio - A collection of securities that provides a balance across several sections of the market. This provides maximum exposure to high returns while minimising risk.

Price-to-Earnings (P/E) ratio - The P/E ratio of a stock is a measure of the price paid for the share relative to the annual income or profit earned by the company per share.

Priority Debts - Priority debts are those where non-payment gives the creditor the right to deprive you of your liberty, home or essential goods and services.

Repayment Mortgage - The monthly repayments paying off both the interest and the capital on the mortgage. During the earlier part of the mortgage term, the majority of the monthly payment goes towards the interest.

Repossession - Process by which a creditor with a loan secured on house or goods (e.g. car) can take possession if you do not maintain agreed payments.

Secured Loan - Where the lender has a legal charge on assets (usually a house) giving rights of repossession over that asset if payments on the loan are not maintained.

Share - A security that represents part-ownership of a company.

Shareholder - If you buy even one share in a company, you can proudly call yourself a shareholder. As a shareholder you get an invitation to the company's annual meeting, and you have the right to vote on the members of the Board of Directors and other company matters.

Standing Order - This is an instruction signed by an account holder ordering a Bank or Building Society to make regular payments from an account of specified amounts on specified dates.

Term Life Insurance - A no-nonsense life insurance plan where you pay low premiums that will increase as you get older. When the term of the insurance comes to an end, you get nothing, except the satisfaction of still being alive.

Unit Trust - A collective investment that pools investors' money, managed by a professional fund manager.

Unsecured Loan - A loan that is not secured on borrower's property or goods.

Warrant of Execution - This is issued by the County Court at the creditor's request allowing the court bailiffs to attempt to take and sell goods and use the proceeds to pay the debt.

Welfare Benefits - State funded allowances paid to those in certain defined circumstances including low income and disability.

About The Author

Niyi Adeoshun, the Money Management Coach, has been involved in developing financial software for Banks, Insurance and Mortgage companies for over two decades. He, however, specialises in inspiring and motivating people to live a life of financial-freedom in order to fulfil their God-given life purposes.

Niyi, who is a Budget Coach to many individuals and families, has spoken to audiences of various sizes and classes. He encourages the subscribers to his Money Management Tips newsletter on a regular basis via email. He uses his YouTube channels to answer various personal finance questions from viewers all over the world.

His books on personal finance like "The Price of Financial Freedom", "Financial Legacy" have, for many years, been a blessing to people all over the world and testimonies are still coming in as to how they are impacting lives for the better.

Niyi lives with his family in Essex, UK.

Other Books by the Author

If you have enjoyed this book, you may want to check out other books by the author.

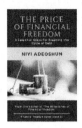

The Price of Financial Freedom
3 Essential Steps For Breaking the Cycle of Debt.

ISBN: 979-8440658028

<u>Winning Together</u>
A Couple's Guide To Success With Money and Marriage

ISBN: 979-8741033074

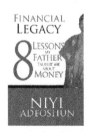

<u>Financial Legacy</u>

8 Lessons My Father Taught Me about Money

ISBN: 978-1530153770

Joshua, Jordan and Jericho

Reaching Beyond All Obstacles to Your Destiny

ISBN: 978-1076576699

The Worship Minister

Pleasing God as We Fulfil His Call

ISBN: 978-1541337206

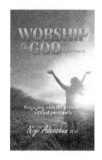

Worship: The God Experience

Engaging With The Presence of God Constantly

ISBN: 978-1533372543

Resources

One of the most widely known things that Niyi does is his email newsletter, called Money Management Tips. Anyone can subscribe by visiting his website. If you subscribe today, there is a special gift waiting for you there:
http://www.niyiadeoshun.com

Niyi loves doing public speaking be it in a school, college, church or other Christian organisations. His talks are a blend of motivation, humour and common-sense using biblical principles. He always challenges his audiences to aim for success through growth in all areas if life. People are informed, educated and somehow entertained. To have Niyi speak to your church, group or function, contact him at: info@niyiadeoshun.com

Niyi guides individuals and families on debt elimination and total financial freedom strategies. He loves working with people who are determined to fulfil their goals and create the life they really want! It is eye-opening, and wonderful things happen!

You can connect with Niyi through these avenues:
Website: http://www.niyiadeoshun.com/
Email: info@niyiadeoshun.com
Twitter: https://twitter.com/niyiadeoshun
Facebook: https://www.facebook.com/MoneyManagementCoach
YouTube Channel: https://www.youtube.com/c/NiyiAdeoshun